KRAFT
PHILADELPHIA

COOKBOOK & RECIPE CARDS

12/25/11

For Paul & Paula,
Bon Appétit!
♡ Jamie

D1400981

Publications
International, Ltd.

Favorite Brand Name Recipes at www.fbnr.com

Louis Weber, CEO
Publications International, Ltd.
7373 North Cicero Avenue
Lincolnwood, IL 60712

Permission is never granted for commercial purposes.

Pictured on the front cover (clockwise from top): Zesty Chicken Pot Pie *(pages 76, 136)*, Creamy Strawberry Cookie "Tarts" *(pages 62, 128)*, Holiday Cheese Truffles *(pages 34, 114)*, *and* New York-Style Sour Cream-Topped Cheesecake *(pages 42, 118)*.

Pictured on the back cover: PHILADELPHIA 3-Step White Chocolate Raspberry Swirl Cheesecake *(pages 18, 104)*.

ISBN-13: 978-1-4127-5864-2
ISBN-10: 1-4127-5864-5

Library of Congress Control Number: 2008941396

Manufactured in China.

8 7 6 5 4 3 2 1

Microwave Cooking: Microwave ovens vary in wattage. Use the cooking times as guidelines and check for doneness before adding more time.

Preparation/Cooking Times: Preparation times are based on the approximate amount of time required to assemble the recipe before cooking, baking, chilling, or serving. These times include preparation steps such as measuring, chopping, and mixing. The fact that some preparations and cooking can be done simultaneously is taken into account. Preparation of optional ingredients and serving suggestions is not included.

Publications
International, Ltd.

Favorite Brand Name Recipes at www.fbnr.com

Contents

PHILADELPHIA CREAM CHEESE
Tips for the Perfect Cheesecake

For best quality and results, always use **PHILADELPHIA** Cream Cheese.

Preheating the oven: The baking time indicated in a recipe is based on using a preheated oven. Turn the oven on when you start to mix the cheesecake ingredients. This should allow enough time for the oven to heat to the correct temperature for when you are ready to place the cheesecake in the oven to bake. Unless otherwise indicated, always bake cheesecakes in the center of the middle oven rack.

Beating the batter: While adding ingredients, do not overbeat the cheesecake batter. Too much air beaten into the batter will result in a cheesecake that sinks in the center when cooled.

Baking cheesecakes: Overbaked cheesecakes tend to crack. Remove the cheesecake from the oven when center is almost set (i.e., center of cheesecake still wiggles when pan is gently shaken from side-to-side). Although the cheesecake appears underbaked, the residual heat in the cheesecake will be enough to finish baking the center. After chilling, the cheesecake will have a perfectly smooth consistency.

White Chocolate Cheesecake

Cooling cheesecakes: Cool cheesecakes completely before refrigerating. Placing a warm cheesecake in the refrigerator will cause condensation to form on the cake, resulting in a soggy cheesecake.

Cutting cheesecakes: Cut cheesecakes when they are cold rather than warm. Use a sharp knife with a clean, thin blade. To make clean cuts, dip the knife in hot water after each cut and wipe the blade clean.

For all of your occasions, **PHILLY MAKES A BETTER CHEESECAKE**.

During tests of plain New York style cheesecake made with PHILADELPHIA Cream Cheese versus store-branded cream cheese, consumers rated PHILLY cheesecake as better tasting.

3-Step Cheesecakes

PHILADELPHIA 3-STEP Coconut Cheesecake

PREP: 10 MIN. PLUS REFRIGERATING • BAKE: 40 MIN.

2 pkg. (8 oz. each) **PHILADELPHIA** Cream Cheese, softened

½ cup cream of coconut

½ cup sugar

½ tsp. vanilla

2 eggs

1 **HONEY MAID** Graham Pie Crust (6 oz.)

2 cups thawed **COOL WHIP** Whipped Topping

½ cup **BAKER'S ANGEL FLAKE** Coconut, toasted

PREHEAT oven to 350°F. Beat cream cheese, cream of coconut, sugar and vanilla with electric mixer on medium speed until well blended. Add eggs; mix just until blended.

POUR into crust.

BAKE 40 min. or until center is almost set. Cool. Refrigerate 3 hours or overnight. Top with whipped topping and toasted coconut just before serving. Store leftover cheesecake in refrigerator.

Makes: 10 servings.

PHILADELPHIA 3-STEP Toffee Crunch Cheesecake

PREP: 10 MIN. PLUS REFRIGERATING • BAKE: 40 MIN.

2 pkg. (8 oz. each)
   PHILADELPHIA Cream Cheese, softened

½ cup firmly packed brown sugar

½ tsp. vanilla

2 eggs

4 chocolate-covered English toffee bars (1.4 oz. each), chopped (about 1 cup), divided

1 **HONEY MAID** Graham Pie Crust (6 oz.)

PREHEAT oven to 350°F. Beat cream cheese, sugar and vanilla in large bowl with electric mixer on medium speed until well blended. Add eggs; mix just until blended. Stir in ¾ cup of the chopped toffee bars.

POUR into crust. Sprinkle with remaining chopped toffee bars.

BAKE 35 to 40 minutes or until center is almost set. Cool. Refrigerate 3 hours or overnight. Store leftover cheesecake in refrigerator.

Makes: 8 servings.

SIZE IT UP: Special recipes are fun to eat as part of an annual celebration. Enjoy a serving of this rich and indulgent dessert at your next family gathering.

GREAT SUBSTITUTE: For extra chocolate flavor, substitute 1 OREO Pie Crust (6 oz.) for the graham pie crust.

PHILADELPHIA 3-STEP Amaretto Berry Cheesecake

PREP: 10 MIN. PLUS REFRIGERATING • BAKE: 40 MIN.

- 2 pkg. (8 oz. each) **PHILADELPHIA** Cream Cheese, softened
- ½ cup sugar
- ½ tsp. vanilla
- 3 Tbsp. almond-flavored liqueur
- 2 eggs
- 1 **HONEY MAID** Graham Pie Crust (6 oz.)
- 2 cups mixed berries (blueberries, raspberries and sliced strawberries)

PREHEAT oven to 350°F. Beat cream cheese, sugar and vanilla in large bowl with electric mixer on medium speed until well blended. Add liqueur; mix well. Add eggs; beat just until blended.

POUR into crust.

BAKE 35 to 40 minutes or until center is almost set. Cool. Refrigerate 3 hours or overnight. Top with berries just before serving. Store leftover cheesecake in refrigerator.

Makes: 8 servings.

SIZE IT UP: This berry cheesecake is the perfect choice for a special occasion. Plan ahead and eat accordingly before indulging in a slice of this cake.

HOW TO SOFTEN CREAM CHEESE: Place completely unwrapped packages of cream cheese on microwaveable plate. Microwave on HIGH 20 seconds or until slightly softened.

GREAT SUBSTITUTE: Prepare as directed, substituting 1 tsp. almond extract for the almond-flavored liqueur.

PHILADELPHIA 3-STEP Crème De Menthe Cheesecake

PREP: 10 MIN. PLUS REFRIGERATING ● BAKE: 40 MIN.

2 pkg. (8 oz. each)
   PHILADELPHIA Cream Cheese, softened

½ cup granulated sugar

½ tsp. vanilla

2 eggs

4 tsp. green crème de menthe

1 **OREO** Pie Crust (6 oz.)

2 tsp. green cake decorating crystals or colored sugar

PREHEAT oven to 350°F. Beat cream cheese, granulated sugar and vanilla with electric mixer on medium speed until well blended. Add eggs; mix well. Stir in crème de menthe.

POUR into crust.

BAKE 40 minutes or until center is almost set. Cool. Refrigerate 3 hours or overnight. Sprinkle with decorating crystals just before serving. Store leftover cheesecake in refrigerator.

Makes: 8 servings.

SIZE IT UP: Enjoy a serving of this rich and indulgent cheesecake on a special occasion.

ALMOND CHERRY CHEESECAKE: Prepare as directed, substituting 2 Tbsp. almond-flavored liqueur for the crème de menthe and using a HONEY MAID Graham Pie Crust. Top with 1 can (21 oz.) cherry pie filling just before serving.

PHILADELPHIA 3-STEP Luscious Lemon Cheesecake

PREP: 10 MIN. PLUS REFRIGERATING • BAKE: 40 MIN.

2 pkg. (8 oz. each)
   PHILADELPHIA Cream Cheese, softened

½ cup sugar

½ tsp. grated lemon peel

1 Tbsp. fresh lemon juice

½ tsp. vanilla

2 eggs

1 **HONEY MAID** Graham Pie Crust (6 oz.)

PREHEAT oven to 350°F. Beat cream cheese, sugar, peel, juice and vanilla with electric mixer on medium speed until well blended. Add eggs; mix just until blended.

POUR into crust.

BAKE 40 min. or until center is almost set. Cool. Refrigerate at least 4 hours. Garnish as desired. Store leftover cheesecake in refrigerator.

Makes: 8 servings.

PHILADELPHIA 3-STEP Cheesecake

PREP: 10 MIN. PLUS REFRIGERATING ● BAKE: 40 MIN.

2 pkg. (8 oz. each)
PHILADELPHIA Cream Cheese, softened

½ cup sugar

½ tsp. vanilla

2 eggs

1 **HONEY MAID** Graham Pie Crust (6 oz.)

PREHEAT oven to 325°F. Beat cream cheese, sugar and vanilla with electric mixer on medium speed until well blended. Add eggs; mix just until blended.

POUR into crust.

BAKE 40 min. or until center is almost set. Cool. Refrigerate 3 hours or overnight. Garnish as desired. Store leftover cheesecake in refrigerator.

Makes: 8 servings.

PHILADELPHIA 3-STEP Cheesecake Bars

PREP: 10 MIN. PLUS REFRIGERATING • BAKE: 40 MIN.

1½ cups **HONEY MAID** Graham Cracker Crumbs

¼ cup (½ stick) butter or margarine, melted

2 pkg. (8 oz. each) **PHILADELPHIA** Cream Cheese, softened

½ cup sugar

½ tsp. vanilla

2 eggs

PREHEAT oven to 350°F. Mix crumbs and butter; press firmly onto bottom of 8- or 9-inch baking pan. Beat cream cheese, sugar and vanilla with electric mixer on medium speed until well blended. Add eggs; mix just until blended. Pour over crust.

BAKE 40 minutes or until center is almost set. Cool.

REFRIGERATE 3 hours or overnight. Cut into 16 bars. Store leftover bars in refrigerator.

Makes: 16 servings, 1 bar each.

SIZE IT UP: Enjoy a serving of this rich and indulgent treat on special occasions.

HOW TO EASILY REMOVE BARS FROM PAN: Line pan with foil before pressing crumb mixture onto bottom of pan.

PHILADELPHIA 3-STEP White Chocolate Raspberry Swirl Cheesecake

PREP: 10 MIN. PLUS REFRIGERATING • BAKE: 40 MIN.

2 pkg. (8 oz. each)
   PHILADELPHIA Cream Cheese,
   softened

½ cup sugar

½ tsp. vanilla

2 eggs

3 squares **BAKER'S** Premium
   White Baking Chocolate,
   melted

1 **OREO** Pie Crust (6 oz.)

3 Tbsp. raspberry preserves

PREHEAT oven to 350°F. Beat cream cheese, sugar and vanilla with electric mixer on medium speed until well blended. Add eggs; mix just until blended. Stir in white chocolate. Pour into crust.

MICROWAVE preserves in small bowl on HIGH 15 sec. or until melted. Dot top of cheesecake with small spoonfuls of preserves. Cut through batter with knife several times for marble effect.

BAKE 35 to 40 min. or until center is almost set. Cool. Refrigerate 3 hours or overnight. Store leftover cheesecake in refrigerator.

Makes: 8 servings.

PHILADELPHIA 3-STEP Cookie Dough Cheesecake

PREP:10 MIN. PLUS REFRIGERATING • BAKE: 40 MIN.

2 pkg. (8 oz. each)
  PHILADELPHIA Cream Cheese,
  softened

½ cup sugar

½ tsp. vanilla

2 eggs

¾ cup prepared or refrigerated
  chocolate chip cookie
  dough, divided

1 **HONEY MAID** Graham Pie
  Crust (6 oz.)

PREHEAT oven to 350°F. Beat cream cheese, sugar and vanilla in large bowl with electric mixer on medium speed until well blended. Add eggs; mix just until blended. Remove ½ cup of the dough; drop by teaspoonfuls into batter. Stir gently.

POUR into crust. Top with level teaspoonfuls of the remaining ¼ cup cookie dough.

BAKE 40 min. or until center is almost set. Cool. Refrigerate 3 hours or overnight. Garnish as desired. Store leftover cheesecake in refrigerator.

Makes: 12 servings.

PHILADELPHIA 3-STEP Mini Cheesecakes

PREP: 10 MIN. PLUS REFRIGERATING

2 pkg. (8 oz. each) **PHILADELPHIA** Cream Cheese, softened

½ cup sugar

½ tsp. vanilla

2 eggs

12 **OREO** Chocolate Sandwich Cookies

1 kiwi, peeled, cut into 6 slices

36 blueberries (about ½ cup)

12 raspberries (about ⅓ cup)

PREHEAT oven to 350°F. Beat cream cheese, sugar and vanilla in large bowl with electric mixer on medium speed until well blended. Add eggs, 1 at a time, beating on low speed after each addition just until blended.

PLACE 1 cookie in bottom of each of 12 medium paper-lined muffin cups. Fill evenly with batter.

BAKE 20 min. or until centers are almost set. Cool. Refrigerate 3 hours or overnight. Cut kiwi slices in half. Top each cheesecake with 1 kiwi half, 3 blueberries and 1 raspberry just before serving.

Makes: 12 servings.

CHEESECAKE SQUARES: Line 8-inch square baking pan with foil. Mix 1½ cups finely crushed OREO Chocolate Sandwich Cookies or HONEY MAID Honey Grahams with ¼ cup melted butter; press firmly onto bottom of pan. Prepare cheesecake batter as directed. Pour over crust. Bake and refrigerate as directed. Cut into 16 squares. Top evenly with the fruit mixture just before serving. Makes 16 servings, 1 square each.

Easy Entertaining

Party Cheese Ball

PREP: 15 MIN. PLUS REFRIGERATING

2   pkg. (8 oz. each) **PHILADELPHIA** Cream Cheese, softened
1   pkg. (8 oz.) **KRAFT** Shredded Sharp Cheddar Cheese
1   Tbsp. finely chopped onions
1   Tbsp. chopped red bell peppers
2   tsp. Worcestershire sauce
1   tsp. lemon juice
    Dash ground red pepper (cayenne)
    Dash salt
1   cup chopped **PLANTERS** Pecans

BEAT cream cheese and Cheddar cheese in small bowl with electric mixer on medium speed until well blended.

MIX in all remaining ingredients except pecans; cover. Refrigerate several hours or overnight.

SHAPE into ball; roll in pecans. Serve with assorted **NABISCO** Crackers.

Makes: 24 servings, 2 Tbsp. each.

PHILLY Shrimp Cocktail Dip

PREP: 10 MIN.

1 pkg. (8 oz.) **PHILADELPHIA** Cream Cheese, softened

¾ lb. cooked shrimp, chopped (about 2 cups)

¾ cup **KRAFT** Cocktail Sauce

¼ cup **KRAFT** Shredded Parmesan Cheese

¼ cup sliced green onions

SPREAD cream cheese onto bottom of 9-inch pie plate. Toss shrimp with cocktail sauce; spoon over cream cheese.

SPRINKLE with Parmesan cheese and onions.

SERVE with **WHEAT THINS** Snack Crackers.

Makes: 3 cups or 24 servings, 2 Tbsp. each.

Blue Cheese Mushrooms

PREP: 30 MIN. • BROIL: 3 MIN.

24	medium fresh mushrooms (1 lb.)
¼	cup sliced green onions
1	Tbsp. butter or margarine
1	pkg. (4 oz.) **ATHENOS** Crumbled Blue Cheese
3	oz. **PHILADELPHIA** Cream Cheese, softened

PREHEAT broiler. Remove stems from mushrooms; chop stems. Cook and stir stems and onions in butter in small skillet on medium heat until tender.

ADD blue cheese and cream cheese; mix well. Spoon evenly into mushroom caps; place on rack of broiler pan.

BROIL 2 to 3 min. or until golden brown. Serve warm.

Makes: 2 dozen or 24 servings, 1 mushroom each.

Cream Cheese Nibbles

PREP: 10 MIN. PLUS REFRIGERATING

1 pkg. (8 oz.) **PHILADELPHIA** Cream Cheese

½ cup **KRAFT** Sun-Dried Tomato Dressing

2 cloves garlic, sliced

3 small sprigs fresh rosemary, stems removed

6 sprigs fresh thyme, cut into pieces

1 tsp. black peppercorns

Peel of 1 lemon, cut into thin strips

CUT cream cheese into 36 pieces. Place in 9-inch pie plate.

ADD remaining ingredients; toss lightly. Cover.

REFRIGERATE at least 1 hour or up to 24 hours. Serve with crusty bread, **NABISCO** Crackers or pita chips.

Makes: 18 servings, 2 pieces each.

Creamy Stuffed Pastry Bites

PREP: 15 MIN. ● BAKE: 15 MIN.

4 oz. (½ of 8-oz. pkg.) **PHILADELPHIA** Cream Cheese, softened

½ cup finely chopped cooked turkey or chicken

2 green onions, sliced

½ tsp. chopped fresh parsley

Salt and black pepper

1 pkg. (17¼ oz.) frozen puff pastry (2 sheets), thawed

1 egg

1 Tbsp. milk

PREHEAT oven to 400°F. Mix cream cheese, turkey, onions and parsley until well blended. Season with salt and pepper to taste.

PLACE pastry sheets on cutting board. Cut out 22 circles from each pastry sheet, using a 2-inch round cutter. Beat egg and milk with wire whisk until well blended.

SPOON 1 tsp. of the turkey mixture onto center of each pastry circle. Brush edge of pastry with egg mixture. Fold pastry in half to completely enclose filling; press edges together to seal. Place on baking sheet; brush tops with remaining egg mixture.

BAKE 12 to 15 min. or until golden brown. Serve immediately.

Makes: 22 servings,
2 pastry bites each.

PHILLY Buffalo Chicken Dip

PREP: 10 MIN.

1 pkg. (8 oz.) **PHILADELPHIA** Cream Cheese, softened

1 pkg. (6 oz.) **OSCAR MAYER** Oven Roasted Chicken Breast Cuts

½ cup Buffalo wing sauce

¼ cup **KRAFT** Natural Blue Cheese Crumbles

¼ cup sliced green onions

SPREAD cream cheese onto bottom of microwaveable 9-inch pie plate. Mix chicken and sauce; spoon over cream cheese. Sprinkle with blue cheese and onions.

MICROWAVE on HIGH 2 min. or until heated through.

SERVE warm with celery sticks and **WHEAT THINS** Snack Crackers.

Makes: 2¼ cups or 18 servings, 2 Tbsp. each.

Creamy Coconut Dip

PREP: 5 MIN. PLUS REFRIGERATING

1 pkg. (8 oz.) **PHILADELPHIA** Cream Cheese, softened

1 can (15 oz.) cream of coconut

1 tub (16 oz.) **COOL WHIP** Whipped Topping, thawed

BEAT cream cheese and cream of coconut in large bowl with wire whisk until well blended.

ADD whipped topping; gently stir until well blended. Cover. Refrigerate several hours or until chilled.

SERVE with **HONEY MAID** Grahams Honey Sticks and cut-up fresh fruit.

Makes: 48 servings, 2 Tbsp. each.

Holiday Cheese Truffles

PREP: 15 MIN.

2 pkg. (8 oz. each) **PHILADELPHIA** Cream Cheese, softened

1 pkg. (8 oz.) **KRAFT** Shredded Sharp Cheddar Cheese

1 tsp. garlic powder

Dash ground red pepper (cayenne)

¼ cup chopped roasted red peppers

2 green onions, sliced

1⅔ cups **PLANTERS** Chopped Pecans

SOCIABLES Savory Crackers

BEAT cream cheese, Cheddar cheese, garlic powder and ground red pepper with electric mixer until blended. Divide in half. Add roasted peppers to half and onions to other half; mix each until blended.

REFRIGERATE several hours or until chilled.

SHAPE into 24 (1-inch) balls. Roll in pecans. Refrigerate until ready to serve.

Makes: 4 doz. truffles or 24 servings, 2 truffles and 5 crackers each.

SIZE-WISE: Enjoy a single serving of this indulgent holiday treat.

SPECIAL EXTRA: Try these other coatings for these tasty truffles: sesame seeds, chopped fresh parsley, paprika and your favorite KRAFT Shredded Cheese.

VARIATIONS: Prepare as directed, using one of the following options: Festive Wreath: Alternately arrange different flavored truffles in a large circle on platter to resemble a holiday wreath. Create a decorative bow out of green onion strips. Use to garnish wreath. Cheese Logs: Roll each half into 6-inch log. Roll in desired coatings as directed.

Pecan Tassies

PREP: 20 MIN. PLUS REFRIGERATING • BAKE: 25 MIN.

4 oz. (½ of 8-oz. pkg.) **PHILADELPHIA** Cream Cheese, softened

½ cup (1 stick) butter or margarine, softened

1 cup all-purpose flour

1 egg

¾ cup firmly packed brown sugar

1 tsp. vanilla

¾ cup finely chopped **PLANTERS** Pecans

3 squares **BAKER'S** Semi-Sweet Baking Chocolate, melted

BEAT cream cheese and butter in large bowl with electric mixer on medium speed until well blended. Add flour; mix well. Cover and refrigerate at least 1 hour or until chilled.

PREHEAT oven to 350°F. Divide dough into 24 balls. Place 1 ball in each of 24 miniature muffin pan cups; press onto bottoms and up sides of cups to form shells. Set aside. Beat egg lightly in small bowl. Add sugar and vanilla; mix well. Stir in pecans. Spoon evenly into pastry shells, filling each shell three-fourths full.

BAKE 25 min. or until lightly browned. Let stand 5 min. in pans; remove to wire racks. Cool completely. Drizzle with melted chocolate. Let stand until set.

Makes: 2 dozen or 24 servings, 1 tart each.

CHIPS AHOY! Cheesecake Sandwiches

PREP: 10 MIN. PLUS REFRIGERATING

4 oz. (½ of 8-oz. pkg.) **PHILADELPHIA** Cream Cheese, softened

2 Tbsp. sugar

1 cup thawed **COOL WHIP** Whipped Topping

20 **CHIPS AHOY!** Real Chocolate Chip Cookies

1 tub (7 oz.) **BAKER'S** Real Milk Dipping Chocolate, melted

BEAT cream cheese and sugar in large bowl with electric mixer on medium speed until well blended. Stir in whipped topping.

COVER bottom (flat) side of each of 10 of the cookies with about 2 Tbsp. of the cream cheese mixture; top each with second cookie, bottom-side down, to form sandwich. Dip half of each sandwich in chocolate; gently shake off excess chocolate. Place in single layer in airtight container.

FREEZE 3 hours or until firm. Store leftover sandwiches in freezer.

Makes: 10 servings,
1 sandwich each.

PHILADELPHIA Dessert Dip

PREP: 5 MIN.

1 pkg. (8 oz.) **PHILADELPHIA** Cream Cheese, softened

1 jar (7 oz.) **JET-PUFFED** Marshmallow Creme

MIX ingredients until well blended; cover.

REFRIGERATE until ready to serve.

SERVE with assorted **NABISCO** Cookies or cut-up fresh fruit.

Makes: 14 servings, 2 Tbsp. each.

MALLOW FRUIT DIP: Add 1 Tbsp. orange juice, 1 tsp. grated orange peel and a dash of ground ginger.

HOW TO SOFTEN CREAM CHEESE: Place completely unwrapped package of cream cheese on microwaveable plate. Microwave on HIGH 10 to 15 seconds or until slightly softened.

MAKE IT EASY: To easily remove marshmallow creme from jar, remove lid and seal. Microwave on HIGH 30 seconds.

Classic Cheesecakes

New York-Style Sour Cream-Topped Cheesecake

PREP: 15 MIN. PLUS REFRIGERATING • BAKE: 40 MIN.

- 1½ cups **HONEY MAID** Graham Cracker Crumbs
- ¼ cup (½ stick) butter, melted
- 1¼ cups sugar, divided
- 4 pkg. (8 oz. each) **PHILADELPHIA** Cream Cheese, softened
- 2 tsp. vanilla, divided
- 1 container (16 oz.) **BREAKSTONE'S** or **KNUDSEN** Sour Cream, divided
- 4 eggs

PREHEAT oven to 325°F. Line 13×9-inch baking pan with foil, with ends of foil extending over sides of pan. Mix crumbs, butter and 2 Tbsp. of the sugar; press firmly onto bottom of prepared pan.

BEAT cream cheese, 1 cup of the remaining sugar and 1 tsp. of the vanilla in large bowl with electric mixer on medium speed until well blended. Add 1 cup of the sour cream; mix well. Add eggs, 1 at a time, beating on low speed after each addition just until blended. Pour over crust.

BAKE 40 min. or until center is almost set. Mix remaining sour cream, 2 Tbsp. sugar and 1 tsp. vanilla until well blended; carefully spread over cheesecake. Bake an additional 10 min. Cool. Cover; refrigerate 4 hours or overnight. Lift cheesecake from pan, using foil handles. Garnish as desired. Store leftover cheesecake in refrigerator.

Makes: 16 servings, 1 piece each.

Tiramisu Cheesecake

PREP: 20 MIN. PLUS REFRIGERATING • BAKE: 45 MIN.

1 box (12 oz.) **NILLA** Wafers (about 88 wafers), divided

5 tsp. **MAXWELL HOUSE** Instant Coffee, divided

3 Tbsp. hot water, divided

4 pkg. (8 oz. each) **PHILADELPHIA** Cream Cheese, softened

1 cup sugar

1 cup **BREAKSTONE'S** or **KNUDSEN** Sour Cream

4 eggs

1 cup thawed **COOL WHIP** Whipped Topping

2 Tbsp. unsweetened cocoa powder

PREHEAT oven to 325°F. Line 13×9-inch baking pan with foil, with ends of foil extending over sides of pan. Layer half of the wafers (about 44) on bottom of prepared pan. Dissolve 2 tsp. of the coffee granules in 2 Tbsp. of the hot water. Brush wafers with half of the dissolved coffee mixture; set remaining aside.

BEAT cream cheese and sugar in large bowl with electric mixer on medium speed until well blended. Add sour cream; mix well. Add eggs, 1 at a time, mixing on low speed after each addition just until blended. Dissolve remaining 3 tsp. coffee granules in remaining 1 Tbsp. hot water. Remove 3½ cups of the batter; place in medium bowl. Stir in dissolved coffee. Pour coffee-flavored batter over wafers in baking pan. Layer remaining wafers over batter. Brush wafers with reserved dissolved coffee. Pour remaining plain batter over wafers.

BAKE 45 min. or until center is almost set. Cool. Refrigerate 3 hours or overnight. Lift cheesecake from pan, using foil handles. Spread with whipped topping; sprinkle with cocoa. Cut into 16 pieces to serve. Store leftover cheesecake in refrigerator.

Makes: 16 servings, 1 piece each.

White Chocolate Cheesecake

PREP: 30 MIN. PLUS REFRIGERATING • BAKE: 1 HOUR

¾ cup sugar, divided

½ cup (1 stick) butter, softened

1½ tsp. vanilla, divided

1 cup all-purpose flour

4 pkg. (8 oz. each) **PHILADELPHIA** Cream Cheese, softened

2 pkg. (6 squares each) **BAKER'S** Premium White Baking Chocolate, melted, slightly cooled

4 eggs

1 pt. (2 cups) raspberries

PREHEAT oven to 325°F if using a silver 9-inch springform pan (or to 300°F if using a dark nonstick 9-inch springform pan). Beat ¼ cup of the sugar, the butter and ½ tsp. of the vanilla in small bowl with electric mixer on medium speed until light and fluffy. Gradually add flour, mixing on low speed until well blended after each addition. Press firmly onto bottom of pan; prick with fork. Bake 25 min. or until edge is lightly browned.

BEAT cream cheese, remaining ½ cup sugar and remaining 1 tsp. vanilla in large bowl with electric mixer on medium speed until well blended. Add melted chocolate; mix well. Add eggs, 1 at a time, beating on low speed after each addition just until blended. Pour over crust.

BAKE 55 min. to 1 hour or until center is almost set. Run knife or metal spatula around rim of pan to loosen cake; cool before removing rim of pan. Refrigerate 4 hours or overnight. Top with the raspberries just before serving. Store leftover cheesecake in refrigerator.

Makes: 16 servings.

Apple Pecan Cheesecake

PREP: 15 MIN. PLUS REFRIGERATING • BAKE: 55 MIN.

1½ cups **HONEY MAID** Graham Cracker Crumbs

¼ cup (½ stick) butter, melted

2 Tbsp. firmly packed brown sugar

4 pkg. (8 oz. each) **PHILADELPHIA** Cream Cheese, softened

1½ cups firmly packed brown sugar, divided

1 tsp. vanilla

1 cup **BREAKSTONE'S** or **KNUDSEN** Sour Cream

4 eggs

4 cups chopped peeled apples (about 3 medium)

¾ cup **PLANTERS** Chopped Pecans

1 tsp. ground cinnamon

PREHEAT oven to 325°F. Line 13×9-inch baking pan with foil, with ends of foil extending over sides of pan. Mix crumbs, butter and 2 Tbsp. brown sugar; press firmly onto bottom of pan.

BEAT cream cheese, 1 cup of the brown sugar and the vanilla in large bowl with electric mixer on medium speed until well blended. Add sour cream; mix well. Add eggs, 1 at a time, mixing on low speed after each addition just until blended. Pour over crust. Mix remaining ½ cup brown sugar, the apples, pecans and cinnamon; spoon evenly over cheesecake batter.

BAKE 55 min. or until center is almost set. Cool. Refrigerate 4 hours or overnight. Let stand at room temperature 30 min. before serving. Lift cheesecake from pan, using foil handles. Cut into 16 pieces. Store leftover cheesecake in refrigerator.

Makes: 16 servings, 1 piece each.

JAZZ IT UP: For an extra special touch, drizzle KRAFT Caramel Topping over each piece of cheesecake just before serving.

BEST OF SEASON: Take advantage of the many varieties of apples that are available. Try using Jonathan, Granny Smith or Honeycrisp for the topping.

HEALTHY LIVING: Looking for ways to save fat and calories? Save 60 calories and 8 grams of fat per serving by preparing as directed, using PHILADELPHIA Neufchâtel Cheese, ⅓ Less Fat than Cream Cheese and BREAKSTONE'S Reduced Fat or KNUDSEN Light Sour Cream.

Chocolate Royale Cheesecake Squares

PREP: 20 MIN. PLUS REFRIGERATING • BAKE: 50 MIN.

24 **OREO** Chocolate Sandwich Cookies, crushed (about 2 cups)

¼ cup (½ stick) butter or margarine, melted

4 pkg. (8 oz. each) **PHILADELPHIA** Cream Cheese, softened

1 cup sugar

2 Tbsp. all-purpose flour

1 tsp. vanilla

1 pkg. (8 squares) **BAKER'S** Semi-Sweet Baking Chocolate, melted, slightly cooled

4 eggs

PREHEAT oven to 325°F. Mix crumbs and butter; press firmly onto bottom of 13×9-inch baking pan. Bake 10 min.

BEAT cream cheese, sugar, flour and vanilla in large bowl with electric mixer on medium speed until well blended. Add melted chocolate; mix well. Add eggs, 1 at a time, mixing on low speed after each addition just until blended. Pour over crust.

BAKE 45 to 50 min. or until center is almost set. Refrigerate at least 4 hours or overnight. Cut into 32 squares to serve. Store leftover dessert squares in refrigerator.

Makes: 32 servings, 1 square each.

Ribbon Bar Cheesecake

PREP: 15 MIN. PLUS REFRIGERATING ● BAKE: 40 MIN.

30 **OREO** Chocolate Sandwich Cookies, crushed

½ cup (1 stick) butter, melted

¼ cup **PLANTERS** Chopped Pecans

¼ cup **BAKER'S ANGEL FLAKE** Coconut

4 pkg. (8 oz. each) **PHILADELPHIA** Cream Cheese, softened

1 cup sugar

4 eggs

½ cup whipping cream

6 squares **BAKER'S** Semi-Sweet Baking Chocolate

PREHEAT oven to 350°F. Mix crushed cookies, butter, pecans and coconut; press firmly onto bottom of 13×9-inch baking pan. Refrigerate while preparing filling.

BEAT cream cheese and sugar in large bowl with electric mixer on medium speed until well blended. Add eggs, 1 at a time, mixing on low speed after each addition just until blended. Pour over crust.

BAKE 40 min. or until center is almost set. Cool. Refrigerate 3 hours or overnight. Place whipping cream and chocolate in saucepan. Cook on low heat until chocolate is completely melted and mixture is well blended, stirring occasionally. Pour over cheesecake. Refrigerate 15 min. or until chocolate is firm. Store leftover cheesecake in refrigerator.

Makes: 16 servings, 1 square each.

SIZE-WISE: This party-size cheesecake is great for large crowds. Be mindful of serving size.

JAZZ IT UP: After chocolate topping is firm, place 1 additional chocolate square in microwaveable bowl. Microwave on MEDIUM 1 min., stirring after 30 seconds. Stir until chocolate is completely melted. Pour into small resealable bag; seal bag. Snip off one small corner from bottom of bag; twist top of bag to squeeze chocolate from bag to pipe a special message, such as "Greetings," on top of cheesecake.

PHILLY Blueberry Swirl Cheesecake

PREP: 15 MIN. PLUS REFRIGERATING • BAKE: 45 MIN.

1 cup **HONEY MAID** Graham Cracker Crumbs

1 cup plus 3 Tbsp. sugar, divided

3 Tbsp. butter or margarine, melted

4 pkg. (8 oz. each) **PHILADELPHIA** Cream Cheese, softened

1 tsp. vanilla

1 cup **BREAKSTONE'S** or **KNUDSEN** Sour Cream

4 eggs

2 cups fresh or thawed frozen blueberries

PREHEAT oven to 325°F. Mix crumbs, 3 Tbsp. of the sugar and the butter. Press firmly onto bottom of foil-lined 13×9-inch baking pan. Bake 10 min.

BEAT cream cheese, remaining 1 cup sugar and the vanilla in large bowl with electric mixer on medium speed until well blended. Add sour cream; mix well. Add eggs, 1 at a time, beating on low speed after each addition just until blended. Pour over crust. Purée the blueberries in a blender or food processor. Gently drop spoonfuls of the puréed blueberries over batter; cut through batter several times with knife for marble effect.

BAKE 45 min. or until center is almost set; cool. Refrigerate at least 4 hours or overnight. Garnish as desired. Store leftover cheesecake in refrigerator.

Makes: 16 servings.

PHILADELPHIA Classic Cheesecake

PREP: 20 MIN. PLUS REFRIGERATING • BAKE: 55 MIN.

1½ cups **HONEY MAID** Graham Cracker Crumbs

3 Tbsp. sugar

⅓ cup butter or margarine, melted

4 pkg. (8 oz. each) **PHILADELPHIA** Cream Cheese, softened

1 cup sugar

1 tsp. vanilla

4 eggs

PREHEAT oven to 325°F if using a silver 9-inch springform pan (or to 300°F if using a dark nonstick springform pan). Mix crumbs, 3 Tbsp. sugar and butter; press firmly onto bottom of pan.

BEAT cream cheese, 1 cup sugar and vanilla with electric mixer on medium speed until well blended. Add eggs, 1 at a time, mixing on low speed after each addition just until blended. Pour over crust.

BAKE 55 min. or until center is almost set. Loosen cake from side of pan; cool before removing side of pan. Refrigerate 4 hours or overnight. Store leftover cheesecake in refrigerator.

Makes: 16 servings.

SIZE IT UP: Sweets can add enjoyment to a balanced diet, but remember to keep tabs on portions.

SPECIAL EXTRA: Top with fresh fruit just before serving.

Our Best Chocolate Cheesecake

PREP: 30 MIN. PLUS REFRIGERATING • BAKE: 55 MIN.

1½ cups crushed **OREO** Chocolate Sandwich Cookies (about 18 cookies)

2 Tbsp. butter or margarine, melted

3 pkg. (8 oz. each) **PHILADELPHIA** Cream Cheese, softened

1 cup sugar

1 tsp. vanilla

1 pkg. (8 squares) **BAKER'S** Semi-Sweet Baking Chocolate, melted, slightly cooled

3 eggs

1 cup thawed **COOL WHIP** Strawberry Whipped Topping

1½ cups assorted seasonal fruit, such as chopped strawberries and sliced kiwi

PREHEAT oven to 325°F if using a silver 9-inch springform pan (or to 300°F if using a dark nonstick 9-inch springform pan). Mix crushed cookies and butter; press firmly onto bottom of pan. Bake 10 min.

BEAT cream cheese, sugar and vanilla with electric mixer on medium speed until well blended. Add chocolate; mix well. Add eggs, 1 at a time, mixing on low speed after each addition just until blended. Pour over crust.

BAKE 45 to 55 min. or until center is almost set. Run knife or metal spatula around rim of pan to loosen cake; cool before removing rim of pan. Refrigerate 4 hours or overnight. Top with whipped topping and fruit.

Makes: 16 servings.

SIZE-WISE: Looking for a special treat? 1 serving of this cheesecake is full of chocolatey flavor.

HOW TO SOFTEN CREAM CHEESE: Place completely unwrapped pkg. of cream cheese in microwaveable bowl. Microwave on HIGH 45 sec. or until slightly softened.

HOW TO: This recipe can also be made in a greased, foil-lined 13×9-inch baking pan. Reduce the baking time by 5 to 10 min.

No-Bake Desserts

PHILADELPHIA Blueberry No-Bake Cheesecake

PREP: 15 MIN. PLUS REFRIGERATING

- 2 cups **HONEY MAID** Graham Cracker Crumbs
- 6 Tbsp. margarine, melted
- 1 cup sugar, divided
- 4 pkg. (8 oz. each) **PHILADELPHIA** Neufchâtel Cheese, ⅓ Less Fat than Cream Cheese, softened
- ½ cup blueberry preserves
- Grated peel from 1 lemon
- 1 pkg. (16 oz.) frozen blueberries, thawed, drained
- 1 tub (8 oz.) **COOL WHIP LITE** Whipped Topping, thawed

MIX graham crumbs, margarine and ¼ cup of the sugar; press firmly onto bottom of 13×9-inch pan. Refrigerate while preparing filling.

BEAT Neufchâtel cheese and remaining ¾ cup sugar in large bowl with electric mixer on medium speed until well blended. Add preserves and lemon peel, mix until blended. Stir in blueberries. Gently stir in whipped topping. Spoon over crust; cover.

REFRIGERATE 4 hours or until firm. Garnish as desired. Store leftovers in refrigerator.

HOW TO MAKE IT WITH FRESH BLUEBERRIES: Place 2 cups blueberries in small bowl with 2 Tbsp. sugar; mash with fork. Add to Neufchâtel cheese mixture; continue as directed.

Makes: 16 servings, 1 piece each.

Creamy Strawberry Cookie "Tarts"

PREP: 15 MIN. PLUS REFRIGERATING

⅔ cup boiling water

1 pkg. (4-serving size) JELL-O Brand Strawberry Flavor Gelatin

1 pkg. (8 oz.) PHILADELPHIA Cream Cheese, cubed

1 cup thawed COOL WHIP Whipped Topping

12 CHIPS AHOY! Real Chocolate Chip Cookies

12 small strawberries

STIR boiling water into dry gelatin mix in small bowl at least 2 min. until completely dissolved. Cool 5 min., stirring occasionally.

POUR gelatin mixture into blender. Add cream cheese; cover. Blend on medium speed 30 to 45 sec. or until well blended; scrape down side of blender container, if needed. Add whipped topping; cover. Blend on low speed 5 sec. or just until blended.

LINE 12 muffin pan cups with paper liners; spray with cooking spray. Place 1 cookie on bottom of each prepared cup; top evenly with the gelatin mixture. Refrigerate 1 hour 30 min. or until firm. Top each with a strawberry just before serving. Store leftover desserts in refrigerator.

Makes: 12 servings.

PHILADELPHIA Chocolate Cheesecakes For Two

PREP: 10 MIN. PLUS REFRIGERATING

2 oz. (¼ of 8-oz. pkg.) **PHILADELPHIA** Cream Cheese, softened

1 Tbsp. sugar

1 square **BAKER'S** Semi-Sweet Baking Chocolate, melted

½ cup thawed **COOL WHIP** Whipped Topping

2 **OREO** Chocolate Sandwich Cookies

BEAT cream cheese, sugar and chocolate in medium bowl with wire whisk until well blended. Add whipped topping; mix well.

PLACE 1 cookie on bottom of each of 2 paper-lined medium muffin cups; fill evenly with cream cheese mixture.

REFRIGERATE 2 hours or overnight. (Or, if you are in a hurry, place in the freezer for 1 hour.)

JAZZ IT UP: Dust surface with cocoa powder. Top with heart-shaped stencil; dust with powdered sugar.

Makes: 2 servings.

Chocolate & Peanut Butter Ribbon Dessert

PREP: 15 MIN. PLUS REFRIGERATING

12 **NUTTER BUTTER** Peanut Butter Sandwich Cookies, divided

2 Tbsp. butter, melted

1 pkg. (8 oz.) **PHILADELPHIA** Cream Cheese, softened

½ cup creamy peanut butter

½ cup sugar

2 tsp. vanilla

1 tub (12 oz.) **COOL WHIP** Whipped Topping, thawed, divided

2 squares **BAKER'S** Semi-Sweet Baking Chocolate, melted

CRUSH 8 of the cookies in resealable plastic bag with rolling pin. Mix cookie crumbs and butter. Press onto bottom of foil-lined 9×5-inch loaf pan.

MIX cream cheese, peanut butter, sugar and vanilla with electric mixer on medium speed until well blended. Gently stir in 3 cups of the whipped topping. Spoon ½ cup of the cream cheese mixture into small bowl. Stir in melted chocolate until well blended; set aside. Spoon half of the remaining cream cheese mixture over crust. Top evenly with chocolate mixture; cover with remaining cream cheese mixture.

FREEZE 4 hours or overnight until firm. Invert onto plate. Remove foil, then re-invert onto serving platter so that crumb layer is on bottom. Coarsely break the remaining 4 cookies. Top dessert with remaining whipping topping and cookies.

Makes: 12 servings.

SIZE-WISE: Savor a serving of this indulgent special-occasion dessert. One loaf makes enough for 12 servings.

HOW TO DOUBLE THE RECIPE: Line 13×9-inch pan with foil, with ends of foil extending over sides of pan; set aside. Prepare recipe as directed, using the 1 tub (12 oz.) whipped topping but increasing the vanilla to 1 Tbsp. and doubling all remaining ingredients. Do not invert dessert to remove from pan but lift dessert from pan using foil handles. Cut into bars to serve.

Tiramisu Bowl

PREP: 20 MIN. PLUS REFRIGERATING

1 pkg. (8 oz.) **PHILADELPHIA** Cream Cheese, softened

3 cups cold milk

2 pkg. (4-serving size each) **JELL-O** Vanilla Flavor Instant Pudding & Pie Filling

1 tub (8 oz.) **COOL WHIP** Whipped Topping, thawed, divided

48 **NILLA** Wafers

½ cup brewed strong **MAXWELL HOUSE** Coffee, cooled

2 squares **BAKER'S** Semi-Sweet Baking Chocolate, coarsely grated

1 cup fresh raspberries

BEAT cream cheese in large bowl with electric mixer until creamy. Gradually beat in milk. Add dry pudding mixes; mix well. Stir in 2 cups of the whipped topping.

LINE bottom and sides of a 2½-qt. bowl with half of the wafers; drizzle with half of the coffee. Layer half of the pudding mixture over wafers, and then top with half of the grated chocolate. Repeat all layers starting with the wafers and coffee. Top with remaining whipped topping and raspberries.

REFRIGERATE at least 2 hours. Store leftovers in refrigerator.

Makes: 16 servings, about ⅔ cup each.

Strawberry Freeze

PREP: 15 MIN. PLUS REFRIGERATING

12 **CHIPS AHOY!** Real Chocolate Chip Cookies

1 pkg. (8 oz.) **PHILADELPHIA** Cream Cheese, softened

½ cup sugar

1 can (12 oz.) frozen berry juice concentrate, thawed

1 cup crushed strawberries

1 tub (8 oz.) **COOL WHIP** Whipped Topping, thawed

2 cups strawberries, halved

ARRANGE cookies in single layer on bottom of 9-inch springform pan; set aside.

BEAT cream cheese and sugar in large bowl with electric mixer on medium speed until well blended. Gradually add juice concentrate, beating well after each addition. Stir in crushed strawberries. Add whipped topping; stir with wire whisk until well blended. Pour over cookies in pan.

FREEZE 6 hours or until firm. Remove from freezer; let stand in refrigerator 15 min. to soften slightly. Top with the halved strawberries just before serving. Store leftover dessert in freezer.

Makes: 16 servings.

SUBSTITUTE: Prepare as directed, using COOL WHIP Strawberry Whipped Topping.

HEALTHY LIVING: Trim 4 grams of fat and 2 grams of saturated fat per serving by preparing with CHIPS AHOY! Reduced Fat Real Chocolate Chip Cookies; PHILADELPHIA Neufchâtel Cheese, ⅓ Less Fat than Cream Cheese and COOL WHIP LITE Whipped Topping.

SUBSTITUTE: Prepare as directed, using your favorite flavor of frozen juice or drink concentrate, such as raspberry, lemonade, grape or pink lemonade.

Fluffy 2-STEP Cheesecake Minis

PREP: 10 MIN. PLUS REFRIGERATING

12 **NILLA** Wafers

1 pkg. (8 oz.) **PHILADELPHIA** Cream Cheese, softened

⅓ cup sugar

1 tub (8 oz.) **COOL WHIP** Whipped Topping, thawed, divided

¼ cup **BAKER'S ANGEL FLAKE** Coconut, toasted

PLACE 1 wafer on bottom of each of 12 paper-lined medium muffin cups; set aside. Beat cream cheese and sugar in large bowl with wire whisk or electric mixer until well blended. Add 2¼ cups of the whipped topping; mix well. Spoon evenly into muffin cups.

REFRIGERATE 3 hours or overnight. Spread tops with remaining whipped topping. Sprinkle with coconut just before serving. Store leftover cheesecakes in refrigerator.

Makes 12 servings,
1 cheesecake each.

Lem'n Berry Cheesecake

PREP: 10 MIN. PLUS REFRIGERATING

1 pkg. (8 oz.) **PHILADELPHIA** Cream Cheese, softened

¼ cup **COUNTRY TIME** Lemonade Flavor Drink Mix

2 Tbsp. sugar

½ cup milk

2 cups thawed **COOL WHIP** Whipped Topping

1 **HONEY MAID** Graham Pie Crust (6 oz.)

1 cup assorted fresh berries

BEAT cream cheese, drink mix and sugar in large bowl until well blended. Gradually add milk, mixing until well blended. Gently stir in whipped topping.

SPOON into crust.

REFRIGERATE 1 hour or until ready to serve. Garnish with berries.

Makes: 8 servings.

GREAT SUBSTITUTE: Prepare as directed, using PHILADELPHIA Neufchâtel Cheese, ⅓ Less Fat than Cream Cheese and COOL WHIP LITE Whipped Topping.

Easy Chocolate Truffles

PREP: 30 MIN. PLUS REFRIGERATING

1 pkg. (8 oz.) **PHILADELPHIA** Cream Cheese, softened

3 cups powdered sugar

1½ pkg. (12 squares) **BAKER'S** Semi-Sweet Baking Chocolate, melted

1½ tsp. vanilla

Suggested coatings: ground **PLANTERS** Walnuts, unsweetened cocoa, powdered sugar and/or **BAKER'S ANGEL FLAKE** Coconut

BEAT cream cheese in large bowl with electric mixer on medium speed until smooth. Gradually add sugar, mixing until well blended.

ADD melted chocolate and vanilla; mix well. Refrigerate 1 hour or until chilled.

SHAPE into 1-inch balls. Roll in walnuts, cocoa, powdered sugar or coconut. Store in refrigerator.

Makes: 24 servings, 3 truffles each.

SIZE-WISE: Put these truffles in pretty fluted candy cups and display on a silver platter for an elegant presentation. Each one is a very special treat. Enjoy a serving after dinner with a cup of freshly brewed coffee.

EASY SPIRITED CHOCOLATE TRUFFLES: Prepare as directed except omit vanilla. Divide truffle mixture into thirds. Add 1 Tbsp. liqueur (almond, coffee or orange-flavored) to each third of mixture; mix well.

Entrées

Zesty Chicken Pot Pie

PREP: 20 MIN. • BAKE: 25 MIN.

12 oz. (1½ pkg. [8 oz. each]) **PHILADELPHIA** Cream Cheese, cubed

½ cup chicken broth

3 cups chopped cooked chicken

2 pkg. (10 oz. each) frozen mixed vegetables, thawed

1 env. **GOOD SEASONS** Italian Salad Dressing & Recipe Mix

1 refrigerated ready-to-use refrigerated pie crust (½ of 15-oz. pkg.)

PREHEAT oven to 425°F. Place cream cheese in large saucepan. Add broth; cook on low heat until cream cheese is completely melted, stirring frequently with wire whisk. Stir in chicken, vegetables and salad dressing mix.

SPOON into 9-inch pie plate. Cover with pie crust; seal and flute edge. Cut several slits in crust to allow steam to escape. Place pie plate on baking sheet.

BAKE 20 to 25 min. or until golden brown.

Makes: 8 servings.

SERVING SUGGESTION: Serve with a mixed green salad and glass of fat-free milk.

MAKE AHEAD: Prepare as directed except for baking. Wrap securely; freeze. When ready to bake, unwrap. Place strips of foil around edge to prevent over browning. Bake frozen pie at 425°F for 1 hour and 10 min. or until heated through.

SUBSTITUTES: Prepare as directed, using PHILADELPHIA Neufchâtel Cheese, ⅓ Less Fat than Cream Cheese, OR GOOD SEASONS Zesty Italian Dressing OR substituting turkey for the chicken.

Family-Favorite Roast Chicken

PREP: 10 MIN. • BAKE: 1 HOUR 30 MIN.

1 (4½-lb.) roasting chicken

¼ tsp. black pepper

⅛ tsp. salt

1 medium lemon, washed

4 oz. (½ of 8-oz. pkg.) **PHILADELPHIA** Cream Cheese, softened

1 Tbsp. Italian seasoning

½ cup **KRAFT** Zesty Italian Dressing

PREHEAT oven to 350°F. Rinse chicken; pat dry with paper towel. Use the tip of a sharp knife to separate the chicken skin from the meat in the chicken breast and tops of the legs. Sprinkle chicken both inside and out with the pepper and salt. Place in 13×9-inch baking dish.

GRATE the lemon; mix the peel with cream cheese and Italian seasoning. Use a small spoon or your fingers to carefully stuff the cream cheese mixture under the chicken skin, pushing the cream cheese mixture carefully toward the legs, being careful to not tear the skin.

CUT the lemon in half; squeeze both halves into small bowl. Add dressing; beat with wire whisk until well blended. Drizzle evenly over chicken. Place the squeezed lemon halves inside the chicken cavity. Insert an ovenproof meat thermometer into thickest part of 1 of the chicken's thighs.

BAKE 1 hour 30 min. or until chicken is no longer pink in center (165°F), basting occasionally with the pan juices.

Makes: 8 servings.

Diner Special Meatloaf

PREP: 15 MIN. • BAKE: 55 MIN.

1 lb. lean ground beef

½ cup **KRAFT** Original Barbecue Sauce

½ cup dry bread crumbs

1 egg, lightly beaten

1¼ cups water

¾ cup milk

2 Tbsp. butter or margarine

½ tsp. salt

1½ cups instant potato flakes

3 oz. **PHILADELPHIA** Cream Cheese, cubed

2 **KRAFT** Singles

PREHEAT oven to 375°F. Mix meat, barbecue sauce, bread crumbs and egg. Shape into loaf in 12×8-inch baking dish.

BAKE 55 minutes. Meanwhile, bring water to boil in medium saucepan. Add milk, butter and salt; stir in potato flakes. Add cream cheese; stir until completely melted.

SPREAD potato mixture over meatloaf; top with Singles. Bake an additional 5 minutes or until Singles begin to melt.

Makes: 4 servings.

ROUND OUT THE MEAL: Serve with a steamed green vegetable, such as green beans, and a whole wheat roll.

GREAT SUBSTITUTE: Substitute 1 pkg. (16 oz.) frozen LOUIS RICH Ground Turkey for the ground beef.

SPECIAL EXTRA: Garnish with chopped fresh chives just before serving.

20-Minute Skillet Salmon

PREP: 10 MIN. • COOK: 10 MIN.

1 Tbsp. oil

4 salmon fillets (1 lb.)

1 cup fat-free milk

½ cup (½ of 8-oz. tub) **PHILADELPHIA** Light Cream Cheese Spread

½ cup chopped cucumbers

2 Tbsp. chopped fresh dill

HEAT oil in large skillet on medium-high heat. Add salmon; cook 5 min. on each side or until salmon flakes easily with fork. Remove from skillet; cover to keep warm.

ADD milk and cream cheese spread to skillet; cook and stir until cream cheese spread is melted and mixture is well blended. Stir in cucumbers and dill.

RETURN salmon to skillet. Cook 2 min. or until heated through. Serve salmon topped with the cream cheese sauce.

Makes: 4 servings.

COOKING KNOW-HOW: When salmon is done, it will appear opaque and flake easily with fork.

FOOD FACTS: Check salmon fillets for bones before cooking by running fingers over surface. Small bumps are usually a sign of bones. Use tweezers to remove any bones.

SUBSTITUTE: Substitute 2 tsp. dill weed for the 2 Tbsp. chopped fresh dill.

Pasta Primavera Alfredo

PREP: 5 MIN. ● COOK: 15 MIN.

4 oz. (½ of 8-oz. pkg.)
   PHILADELPHIA Cream Cheese,
   cubed

¾ cup milk

½ cup **KRAFT** Shredded
   Parmesan Cheese

¼ cup (½ stick) butter or
   margarine

¼ tsp. white pepper

¼ tsp. garlic powder

⅛ tsp. ground nutmeg

2 cups small broccoli florets

1 cup chopped carrots

1 pkg. (9 oz.) refrigerated
   fettuccine

PLACE cream cheese, milk, Parmesan cheese and butter in small saucepan; cook on medium-low heat until cream cheese is completely melted and mixture is well blended, stirring occasionally. Add pepper, garlic powder and nutmeg; stir until well blended.

MEANWHILE, add vegetables and pasta to 2½ qt. boiling water in large saucepan; cook 3 min. Drain.

TOSS pasta mixture with the cream cheese mixture.

Makes: 5 servings, 1¼ cups each.

Stuffed Fiesta Burgers

PREP: 15 MIN. • GRILL: 9 MIN.

1 lb. ground beef

1 pkg. (1¼ oz.) **TACO BELL®
HOME ORIGINALS®** Taco
Seasoning Mix

¼ cup **PHILADELPHIA** Chive &
Onion Cream Cheese Spread

⅓ cup **KRAFT** Shredded Cheddar
Cheese

4 hamburger buns, split,
lightly toasted

½ cup **TACO BELL® HOME
ORIGINALS®** Thick 'N Chunky
Medium Salsa

1 avocado, peeled, pitted and
cut into 8 slices

PREHEAT grill to medium heat. Mix meat and seasoning mix. Shape into 8 thin patties. Mix cream cheese spread and shredded cheese. Spoon about 2 Tbsp. of the cheese mixture onto center of each of 4 of the patties; top with second patty. Pinch edges of patties together to seal.

GRILL 7 to 9 min. on each side or until cooked through (160°F).

COVER bottom halves of buns with burgers. Top with salsa, avocado slices and top halves of buns.

Makes: 4 servings, 1 burger each.

TACO BELL® and HOME ORIGINALS® are trademarks owned and licensed by Taco Bell Corp.

Creamy Bow-Tie Pasta With Chicken And Broccoli

PREP: 10 MIN. • COOK: 15 MIN.

3 cups (8 oz.) farfalle (bow-tie pasta), uncooked

4 cups broccoli florets

3 Tbsp. **KRAFT** Roasted Red Pepper Italian with Parmesan Dressing

6 small boneless, skinless chicken breast halves (1½ lb.)

2 cloves garlic, minced

2 cups tomato-basil spaghetti sauce

4 oz. (½ of 8-oz. pkg.) **PHILADELPHIA** Neufchâtel Cheese, ⅓ Less Fat than Cream Cheese, cubed

¼ cup **KRAFT** 100% Grated Parmesan Cheese

COOK pasta as directed on package, adding broccoli to the cooking water for the last 3 min. of the pasta cooking time. Meanwhile, heat dressing in large nonstick skillet on medium heat. Add chicken and garlic; cook 5 min. Turn chicken over; continue cooking 4 to 5 min. or until chicken is cooked through (170°F).

DRAIN pasta mixture in colander; return to pan and set aside. Add spaghetti sauce and Neufchâtel cheese to chicken in skillet; cook on medium-low heat 2 to 3 min. or until Neufchâtel cheese is completely melted, mixture is well blended and chicken is coated with sauce, stirring occasionally. Remove chicken from skillet; keep warm. Add sauce mixture to pasta mixture; mix well. Transfer to 6 serving bowls.

CUT chicken crosswise into thick slices; fan out chicken over pasta mixture. Sprinkle evenly with Parmesan cheese.

Makes: 6 servings, about 1½ cups each.

SUBSTITUTE: Prepare as directed, using whole wheat or multigrain pasta.

Spaghetti With Zesty Bolognese

PREP: 10 MIN. • COOK: 15 MIN.

1 small onion, chopped

¼ cup **KRAFT** Light Zesty Italian Reduced Fat Dressing

1 lb. extra lean ground beef

1 can (15 oz.) tomato sauce

1 can (14 oz.) diced tomatoes, undrained

2 Tbsp. **PHILADELPHIA** Neufchâtel Cheese, ⅓ Less Fat than Cream Cheese

12 oz. spaghetti, uncooked

¼ cup **KRAFT** 100% Grated Parmesan Cheese

COOK onions in dressing in large skillet on medium heat. Increase heat to medium-high. Add meat; cook, stirring frequently, until browned. Stir in tomato sauce and tomatoes. Bring to boil. Reduce heat to medium-low; simmer 15 min. Remove from heat. Stir in Neufchâtel cheese until well blended.

MEANWHILE, cook pasta as directed on package.

SPOON sauce over pasta. Sprinkle with Parmesan cheese.

Makes: 6 servings.

Chicken Enchiladas

PREP: 20 MIN. • BAKE: 20 MIN.

2 cups chopped cooked chicken or turkey

1 green bell pepper, chopped

4 oz. (½ of 8-oz. pkg.) **PHILADELPHIA** Cream Cheese, cubed

½ cup **TACO BELL® HOME ORIGINALS®** Thick 'N Chunky Salsa, divided

8 **TACO BELL® HOME ORIGINALS®** Flour Tortillas

¼ lb. (4 oz.) **VELVEETA** Pasteurized Prepared Cheese Product, cut into ½-inch cubes

1 Tbsp. milk

PREHEAT oven to 350°F. Mix chicken, green bell pepper, cream cheese and ¼ cup of the salsa in saucepan; cook on low heat until cream cheese is melted, stirring occasionally.

SPOON ⅓ cup of the chicken mixture down center of each tortilla; roll up. Place, seam-sides down, in lightly greased 13×9-inch baking dish. Place **VELVEETA** in small saucepan. Add milk; cook on low heat until **VELVEETA** is completely melted, stirring frequently. Pour over enchiladas; cover with foil.

BAKE 20 min. or until heated through. Top with remaining ¼ cup salsa.

Makes: 4 servings, 2 enchiladas each.

TACO BELL® and HOME ORIGINALS® are trademarks owned and licensed by Taco Bell Corp.

SUBSTITUTE: Prepare as directed, using PHILADELPHIA Neufchâtel Cheese, ⅓ Less Fat than Cream Cheese and VELVEETA Made With 2% Milk Reduced Fat Pasteurized Prepared Cheese Product.

SHORTCUT: Substitute 1 pkg. (6 oz.) OSCAR MAYER Oven Roasted Chicken Breast Cuts for the chopped cooked fresh chicken.

METRIC CONVERSION CHART

VOLUME MEASUREMENTS (dry)

1/8 teaspoon = 0.5 mL
1/4 teaspoon = 1 mL
1/2 teaspoon = 2 mL
3/4 teaspoon = 4 mL
1 teaspoon = 5 mL
1 tablespoon = 15 mL
2 tablespoons = 30 mL
1/4 cup = 60 mL
1/3 cup = 75 mL
1/2 cup = 125 mL
2/3 cup = 150 mL
3/4 cup = 175 mL
1 cup = 250 mL
2 cups = 1 pint = 500 mL
3 cups = 750 mL
4 cups = 1 quart = 1 L

VOLUME MEASUREMENTS (fluid)

1 fluid ounce (2 tablespoons) = 30 mL
4 fluid ounces (1/2 cup) = 125 mL
8 fluid ounces (1 cup) = 250 mL
12 fluid ounces (1 1/2 cups) = 375 mL
16 fluid ounces (2 cups) = 500 mL

WEIGHTS (mass)

1/2 ounce = 15 g
1 ounce = 30 g
3 ounces = 90 g
4 ounces = 120 g
8 ounces = 225 g
10 ounces = 285 g
12 ounces = 360 g
16 ounces = 1 pound = 450 g

DIMENSIONS

1/16 inch = 2 mm
1/8 inch = 3 mm
1/4 inch = 6 mm
1/2 inch = 1.5 cm
3/4 inch = 2 cm
1 inch = 2.5 cm

OVEN TEMPERATURES

250°F = 120°C
275°F = 140°C
300°F = 150°C
325°F = 160°C
350°F = 180°C
375°F = 190°C
400°F = 200°C
425°F = 220°C
450°F = 230°C

BAKING PAN SIZES

Utensil	Size in Inches/Quarts	Metric Volume	Size in Centimeters
Baking or	8×8×2	2 L	20×20×5
Cake Pan	9×9×2	2.5 L	23×23×5
(square or	12×8×2	3 L	30×20×5
rectangular)	13×9×2	3.5 L	33×23×5
Loaf Pan	8×4×3	1.5 L	20×10×7
	9×5×3	2 L	23×13×7
Round Layer	8×1½	1.2 L	20×4
Cake Pan	9×1½	1.5 L	23×4
Pie Plate	8×1¼	750 mL	20×3
	9×1¼	1 L	23×3
Baking Dish	1 quart	1 L	—
or Casserole	1½ quarts	1.5 L	—
	2 quarts	2 L	—

PHILADELPHIA 3-STEP Coconut Cheesecake

PHILADELPHIA 3-STEP Toffee Crunch Cheesecake

PHILADELPHIA 3-STEP Coconut Cheesecake

PREP: 10 MIN. PLUS REFRIGERATING • BAKE: 40 MIN.

2 pkg. (8 oz. each) **PHILADELPHIA** Cream Cheese, softened
½ cup cream of coconut
½ cup sugar
½ tsp. vanilla
2 eggs
1 **HONEY MAID** Graham Pie Crust (6 oz.)
2 cups thawed **COOL WHIP** Whipped Topping
½ cup **BAKER'S ANGEL FLAKE** Coconut, toasted

PREHEAT oven to 350°F. Beat cream cheese, cream of coconut, sugar and vanilla with electric mixer on medium speed until well blended. Add eggs; mix just until blended.

POUR into crust.

BAKE 40 min. or until center is almost set. Cool. Refrigerate 3 hours or overnight. Top with whipped topping and toasted coconut just before serving. Store leftover cheesecake in refrigerator.

Makes: 10 servings.

PHILADELPHIA 3-STEP Toffee Crunch Cheesecake

PREP: 10 MIN. PLUS REFRIGERATING • BAKE: 40 MIN.

2 pkg. (8 oz. each) **PHILADELPHIA** Cream Cheese, softened
½ cup firmly packed brown sugar
½ tsp. vanilla
2 eggs
4 chocolate-covered English toffee bars (1.4 oz. each), chopped (about 1 cup), divided
1 **HONEY MAID** Graham Pie Crust (6 oz.)

PREHEAT oven to 350°F. Beat cream cheese, sugar and vanilla in large bowl with electric mixer on medium speed until well blended. Add eggs; mix just until blended. Stir in ¾ cup of the chopped toffee bars.

POUR into crust. Sprinkle with remaining chopped toffee bars.

BAKE 35 to 40 minutes or until center is almost set. Cool. Refrigerate 3 hours or overnight. Store leftover cheesecake in refrigerator.

Makes: 8 servings.

SIZE IT UP: Special recipes are fun to eat as part of an annual celebration. Enjoy a serving of this rich and indulgent dessert at your next family gathering.

GREAT SUBSTITUTE: For extra chocolate flavor, substitute 1 OREO Pie Crust (6 oz.) for the graham pie crust.

PHILADELPHIA 3-STEP Amaretto Berry Cheesecake

PHILADELPHIA 3-STEP Crème De Menthe Cheesecake

PHILADELPHIA 3-STEP Amaretto Berry Cheesecake

PREP: 10 MIN. PLUS REFRIGERATING • BAKE: 40 MIN.

2 pkg. (8 oz. each) **PHILADELPHIA** Cream Cheese, softened
½ cup sugar
½ tsp. vanilla
3 Tbsp. almond-flavored liqueur
2 eggs
1 **HONEY MAID** Graham Pie Crust (6 oz.)
2 cups mixed berries (blueberries, raspberries and sliced strawberries)

PREHEAT oven to 350°F. Beat cream cheese, sugar and vanilla in large bowl with electric mixer on medium speed until well blended. Add liqueur; mix well. Add eggs; beat just until blended.

POUR into crust.

BAKE 35 to 40 minutes or until center is almost set. Cool. Refrigerate 3 hours or overnight. Top with berries just before serving. Store leftover cheesecake in refrigerator.

Makes: 8 servings.

SIZE IT UP: This berry cheesecake is the perfect choice for a special occasion. Plan ahead and eat accordingly before indulging in a slice of this cake.

HOW TO SOFTEN CREAM CHEESE: Place completely unwrapped packages of cream cheese on microwaveable plate. Microwave on HIGH 20 seconds or until slightly softened.

GREAT SUBSTITUTE: Prepare as directed, substituting 1 tsp. almond extract for the almond-flavored liqueur.

PHILADELPHIA 3-STEP Crème De Menthe Cheesecake

PREP: 10 MIN. PLUS REFRIGERATING • BAKE: 40 MIN.

2 pkg. (8 oz. each) **PHILADELPHIA** Cream Cheese, softened
½ cup granulated sugar
½ tsp. vanilla
2 eggs
4 tsp. green crème de menthe
1 **OREO** Pie Crust (6 oz.)
2 tsp. green cake decorating crystals or colored sugar

PREHEAT oven to 350°F. Beat cream cheese, granulated sugar and vanilla with electric mixer on medium speed until well blended. Add eggs; mix well. Stir in crème de menthe.

POUR into crust.

BAKE 40 minutes or until center is almost set. Cool. Refrigerate 3 hours or overnight. Sprinkle with decorating crystals just before serving. Store leftover cheesecake in refrigerator.

Makes: 8 servings.

SIZE IT UP: Enjoy a serving of this rich and indulgent cheesecake on a special occasion.

ALMOND CHERRY CHEESECAKE: Prepare as directed, substituting 2 Tbsp. almond-flavored liqueur for the crème de menthe and using a HONEY MAID Graham Pie Crust. Top with 1 can (21 oz.) cherry pie filling just before serving.

PHILADELPHIA 3-STEP Luscious Lemon Cheesecake

PHILADELPHIA 3-STEP Cheesecake

PHILADELPHIA 3-STEP Luscious Lemon Cheesecake

PREP: 10 MIN. PLUS REFRIGERATING • BAKE: 40 MIN.

2 pkg. (8 oz. each) **PHILADELPHIA** Cream Cheese, softened
½ cup sugar
½ tsp. grated lemon peel
1 Tbsp. fresh lemon juice
½ tsp. vanilla
2 eggs
1 **HONEY MAID** Graham Pie Crust (6 oz.)

PREHEAT oven to 350°F. Beat cream cheese, sugar, peel, juice and vanilla with electric mixer on medium speed until well blended. Add eggs; mix just until blended.

POUR into crust.

BAKE 40 min. or until center is almost set. Cool. Refrigerate at least 4 hours. Garnish as desired. Store leftover cheesecake in refrigerator.

Makes: 8 servings.

PHILADELPHIA 3-STEP Cheesecake

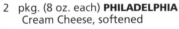

PREP: 10 MIN. PLUS REFRIGERATING • BAKE: 40 MIN.

2 pkg. (8 oz. each) **PHILADELPHIA** Cream Cheese, softened
½ cup sugar
½ tsp. vanilla
2 eggs
1 **HONEY MAID** Graham Pie Crust (6 oz.)

PREHEAT oven to 325°F. Beat cream cheese, sugar and vanilla with electric mixer on medium speed until well blended. Add eggs; mix just until blended.

POUR into crust.

BAKE 40 min. or until center is almost set. Cool. Refrigerate 3 hours or overnight. Garnish as desired. Store leftover cheesecake in refrigerator.

Makes: 8 servings.

PHILADELPHIA 3-STEP Cheesecake Bars

PHILADELPHIA 3-STEP White Chocolate Raspberry Swirl Cheesecake

PHILADELPHIA 3-STEP Cheesecake Bars

PREP: 10 MIN. PLUS REFRIGERATING • BAKE: 40 MIN.

1½ cups **HONEY MAID** Graham Cracker
Crumbs

¼ cup (½ stick) butter or margarine,
melted

2 pkg. (8 oz. each) **PHILADELPHIA**
Cream Cheese, softened

½ cup sugar

½ tsp. vanilla

2 eggs

PREHEAT oven to 350°F. Mix crumbs and butter; press firmly onto bottom of 8- or 9-inch baking pan. Beat cream cheese, sugar and vanilla with electric mixer on medium speed until well blended. Add eggs; mix just until blended. Pour over crust.

BAKE 40 minutes or until center is almost set. Cool.

REFRIGERATE 3 hours or overnight. Cut into 16 bars. Store leftover bars in refrigerator.

Makes: 16 servings, 1 bar each.

SIZE IT UP: Enjoy a serving of this rich and indulgent treat on special occasions.

HOW TO EASILY REMOVE BARS FROM PAN: Line pan with foil before pressing crumb mixture onto bottom of pan.

PHILADELPHIA 3-STEP White Chocolate Raspberry Swirl Cheesecake

PREP: 10 MIN. PLUS REFRIGERATING • BAKE: 40 MIN.

2 pkg. (8 oz. each) **PHILADELPHIA**
Cream Cheese, softened

½ cup sugar

½ tsp. vanilla

2 eggs

3 squares **BAKER'S** Premium White
Baking Chocolate, melted

1 **OREO** Pie Crust (6 oz.)

3 Tbsp. raspberry preserves

PREHEAT oven to 350°F. Beat cream cheese, sugar and vanilla with electric mixer on medium speed until well blended. Add eggs; mix just until blended. Stir in white chocolate. Pour into crust.

MICROWAVE preserves in small bowl on HIGH 15 sec. or until melted. Dot top of cheesecake with small spoonfuls of preserves. Cut through batter with knife several times for marble effect.

BAKE 35 to 40 min. or until center is almost set. Cool. Refrigerate 3 hours or overnight. Store leftover cheesecake in refrigerator.

Makes: 8 servings.

PHILADELPHIA 3-STEP Cookie Dough Cheesecake

PHILADELPHIA 3-STEP Mini Cheesecakes

PHILADELPHIA 3-STEP Cookie Dough Cheesecake

PREP: 10 MIN. PLUS REFRIGERATING • BAKE: 40 MIN.

2 pkg. (8 oz. each) **PHILADELPHIA** Cream Cheese, softened
½ cup sugar
½ tsp. vanilla
2 eggs
¾ cup prepared or refrigerated chocolate chip cookie dough, divided
1 **HONEY MAID** Graham Pie Crust (6 oz.)

PREHEAT oven to 350°F. Beat cream cheese, sugar and vanilla in large bowl with electric mixer on medium speed until well blended. Add eggs; mix just until blended. Remove ½ cup of the dough; drop by teaspoonfuls into batter. Stir gently.

POUR into crust. Top with level teaspoonfuls of the remaining ¼ cup cookie dough.

BAKE 40 min. or until center is almost set. Cool. Refrigerate 3 hours or overnight. Garnish as desired. Store leftover cheesecake in refrigerator.

Makes: 12 servings.

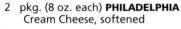

PHILADELPHIA 3-STEP Mini Cheesecakes

PREP: 10 MIN. PLUS REFRIGERATING • BAKE: 20 MIN.

2 pkg. (8 oz. each) **PHILADELPHIA** Cream Cheese, softened
½ cup sugar
½ tsp. vanilla
2 eggs
12 **OREO** Chocolate Sandwich Cookies
1 kiwi, peeled, cut into 6 slices
36 blueberries (about ½ cup)
12 raspberries (about ⅓ cup)

PREHEAT oven to 350°F. Beat cream cheese, sugar and vanilla in large bowl with electric mixer on medium speed until well blended. Add eggs, 1 at a time, beating on low speed after each addition just until blended.

PLACE 1 cookie in bottom of each of 12 medium paper-lined muffin cups. Fill evenly with batter.

BAKE 20 min. or until centers are almost set. Cool. Refrigerate 3 hours or overnight. Cut kiwi slices in half. Top each cheesecake with 1 kiwi half, 3 blueberries and 1 raspberry just before serving.

Makes: 12 servings.

CHEESECAKE SQUARES: Line 8-inch square baking pan with foil. Mix 1½ cups finely crushed OREO Chocolate Sandwich Cookies or HONEY MAID Honey Grahams with ¼ cup melted butter; press firmly onto bottom of pan. Prepare cheesecake batter as directed. Pour over crust. Bake and refrigerate as directed. Cut into 16 squares. Top evenly with the fruit mixture just before serving. Makes 16 servings, 1 square each.

Party Cheese Ball

PHILLY Shrimp Cocktail Dip

Party Cheese Ball

PREP: 15 MIN. PLUS REFRIGERATING

2 pkg. (8 oz. each) **PHILADELPHIA** Cream Cheese, softened
1 pkg. (8 oz.) **KRAFT** Shredded Sharp Cheddar Cheese
1 Tbsp. finely chopped onions
1 Tbsp. chopped red bell peppers
2 tsp. Worcestershire sauce
1 tsp. lemon juice
Dash ground red pepper (cayenne)
Dash salt
1 cup chopped **PLANTERS** Pecans

BEAT cream cheese and Cheddar cheese in small bowl with electric mixer on medium speed until well blended.

MIX in all remaining ingredients except pecans; cover. Refrigerate several hours or overnight.

SHAPE into ball; roll in pecans. Serve with assorted **NABISCO** Crackers.

Makes: 24 servings, 2 Tbsp. each.

PHILLY Shrimp Cocktail Dip

PREP: 10 MIN.

1 pkg. (8 oz.) **PHILADELPHIA** Cream Cheese, softened
¾ lb. cooked shrimp, chopped (about 2 cups)
¾ cup **KRAFT** Cocktail Sauce
¼ cup **KRAFT** Shredded Parmesan Cheese
¼ cup sliced green onions

SPREAD cream cheese onto bottom of 9-inch pie plate. Toss shrimp with cocktail sauce; spoon over cream cheese.

SPRINKLE with Parmesan cheese and onions.

SERVE with **WHEAT THINS** Snack Crackers.

Makes: 3 cups or 24 servings, 2 Tbsp. each.

Blue Cheese Mushrooms

Cream Cheese Nibbles

Blue Cheese Mushrooms

PREP: 30 MIN. • BROIL: 3 MIN.

24 medium fresh mushrooms
   (1 lb.)
¼ cup sliced green onions
1 Tbsp. butter or margarine
1 pkg. (4 oz.) **ATHENOS** Crumbled Blue
   Cheese
3 oz. **PHILADELPHIA** Cream Cheese,
   softened

PREHEAT broiler. Remove stems from mushrooms; chop stems. Cook and stir stems and onions in butter in small skillet on medium heat until tender.

ADD blue cheese and cream cheese; mix well. Spoon evenly into mushroom caps; place on rack of broiler pan.

BROIL 2 to 3 min. or until golden brown. Serve warm.

*Makes: 2 dozen or 24 servings,
1 mushroom each.*

Cream Cheese Nibbles

PREP: 10 MIN. PLUS REFRIGERATING

1 pkg. (8 oz.) **PHILADELPHIA** Cream
   Cheese
½ cup **KRAFT** Sun-Dried Tomato
   Dressing
2 cloves garlic, sliced
3 small sprigs fresh rosemary, stems
   removed
6 sprigs fresh thyme, cut into pieces
1 tsp. black peppercorns
   Peel of 1 lemon, cut into thin strips

CUT cream cheese into 36 pieces. Place in 9-inch pie plate.

ADD remaining ingredients; toss lightly. Cover.

REFRIGERATE at least 1 hour or up to 24 hours. Serve with crusty bread, **NABISCO** Crackers or pita chips.

Makes: 18 servings, 2 pieces each.

Creamy Stuffed Pastry Bites

PHILLY Buffalo Chicken Dip

Creamy Stuffed Pastry Bites

PREP: 15 MIN. • BAKE: 15 MIN.

4 oz. (½ of 8-oz. pkg.) **PHILADELPHIA** Cream Cheese, softened
½ cup finely chopped cooked turkey or chicken
2 green onions, sliced
½ tsp. chopped fresh parsley
Salt and black pepper
1 pkg. (17¼ oz.) frozen puff pastry (2 sheets), thawed
1 egg
1 Tbsp. milk

PREHEAT oven to 400°F. Mix cream cheese, turkey, onions and parsley until well blended. Season with salt and pepper to taste.

PLACE pastry sheets on cutting board. Cut out 22 circles from each pastry sheet, using a 2-inch round cutter. Beat egg and milk with wire whisk until well blended.

SPOON 1 tsp. of the turkey mixture onto center of each pastry circle. Brush edge of pastry with egg mixture. Fold pastry in half to completely enclose filling; press edges together to seal. Place on baking sheet; brush tops with remaining egg mixture.

BAKE 12 to 15 min. or until golden brown. Serve immediately.

Makes: 22 servings, 2 pastry bites each.

PHILLY Buffalo Chicken Dip

PREP: 10 MIN.

1 pkg. (8 oz.) **PHILADELPHIA** Cream Cheese, softened
1 pkg. (6 oz.) **OSCAR MAYER** Oven Roasted Chicken Breast Cuts
½ cup Buffalo wing sauce
¼ cup **KRAFT** Natural Blue Cheese Crumbles
¼ cup sliced green onions

SPREAD cream cheese onto bottom of microwaveable 9-inch pie plate. Mix chicken and sauce; spoon over cream cheese. Sprinkle with blue cheese and onions.

MICROWAVE on HIGH 2 min. or until heated through.

SERVE warm with celery sticks and **WHEAT THINS** Snack Crackers.

Makes: 2¼ cups or 18 servings, 2 Tbsp. each.

Creamy Coconut Dip

Holiday Cheese Truffles

Creamy Coconut Dip

PREP: 5 MIN. PLUS REFRIGERATING

1 pkg. (8 oz.) **PHILADELPHIA** Cream Cheese, softened
1 can (15 oz.) cream of coconut
1 tub (16 oz.) **COOL WHIP** Whipped Topping, thawed

BEAT cream cheese and cream of coconut in large bowl with wire whisk until well blended.

ADD whipped topping; gently stir until well blended. Cover. Refrigerate several hours or until chilled.

SERVE with **HONEY MAID** Grahams Honey Sticks and cut-up fresh fruit.

Makes: 48 servings, 2 Tbsp. each.

Holiday Cheese Truffles

PREP: 15 MIN.

2 pkg. (8 oz. each) **PHILADELPHIA** Cream Cheese, softened
1 pkg. (8 oz.) **KRAFT** Shredded Sharp Cheddar Cheese
1 tsp. garlic powder
Dash ground red pepper (cayenne)
¼ cup chopped roasted red peppers
2 green onions, sliced
1⅔ cups **PLANTERS** Chopped Pecans
SOCIABLES Savory Crackers

BEAT cream cheese, Cheddar cheese, garlic powder and ground red pepper with electric mixer until blended. Divide in half. Add roasted peppers to half and onions to other half; mix each until blended.

REFRIGERATE several hours or until chilled.

SHAPE into 24 (1-inch) balls. Roll in pecans. Refrigerate until ready to serve.

Makes: 4 doz. truffles or 24 servings, 2 truffles and 5 crackers each.

SIZE-WISE: Enjoy a single serving of this indulgent holiday treat.

SPECIAL EXTRA: Try these other coatings for these tasty truffles: sesame seeds, chopped fresh parsley, paprika and your favorite KRAFT Shredded Cheese.

VARIATIONS: Prepare as directed, using one of the following options: Festive Wreath: Alternately arrange different flavored truffles in a large circle on platter to resemble a holiday wreath. Create a decorative bow out of green onion strips. Use to garnish wreath. Cheese Logs: Roll each half into 6-inch log. Roll in desired coatings as directed.

Pecan Tassies

CHIPS AHOY! Cheesecake Sandwiches

Pecan Tassies

PREP: 20 MIN. PLUS REFRIGERATING • BAKE: 25 MIN.

4 oz. (½ of 8-oz. pkg.) **PHILADELPHIA** Cream Cheese, softened
½ cup (1 stick) butter or margarine, softened
1 cup all-purpose flour
1 egg
¾ cup firmly packed brown sugar
1 tsp. vanilla
¾ cup finely chopped **PLANTERS** Pecans
3 squares **BAKER'S** Semi-Sweet Baking Chocolate, melted

BEAT cream cheese and butter in large bowl with electric mixer on medium speed until well blended. Add flour; mix well. Cover and refrigerate at least 1 hour or until chilled.

PREHEAT oven to 350°F. Divide dough into 24 balls. Place 1 ball in each of 24 miniature muffin pan cups; press onto bottoms and up sides of cups to form shells. Set aside. Beat egg lightly in small bowl. Add sugar and vanilla; mix well. Stir in pecans. Spoon evenly into pastry shells, filling each shell three-fourths full.

BAKE 25 min. or until lightly browned. Let stand 5 min. in pans; remove to wire racks. Cool completely. Drizzle with melted chocolate. Let stand until set.

Makes: 2 dozen or 24 servings, 1 tart each.

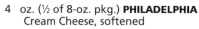

CHIPS AHOY! Cheesecake Sandwiches

PREP: 10 MIN. PLUS REFRIGERATING

4 oz. (½ of 8-oz. pkg.) **PHILADELPHIA** Cream Cheese, softened
2 Tbsp. sugar
1 cup thawed **COOL WHIP** Whipped Topping
20 **CHIPS AHOY!** Real Chocolate Chip Cookies
1 tub (7 oz.) **BAKER'S** Real Milk Dipping Chocolate, melted

BEAT cream cheese and sugar in large bowl with electric mixer on medium speed until well blended. Stir in whipped topping.

COVER bottom (flat) side of each of 10 of the cookies with about 2 Tbsp. of the cream cheese mixture; top each with second cookie, bottom-side down, to form sandwich. Dip half of each sandwich in chocolate; gently shake off excess chocolate. Place in single layer in airtight container.

FREEZE 3 hours or until firm. Store leftover sandwiches in freezer.

Makes: 10 servings, 1 sandwich each.

PHILADELPHIA Dessert Dip

New York-Style Sour Cream-Topped Cheesecake

PHILADELPHIA Dessert Dip

PREP: 5 MIN.

1 pkg. (8 oz.) **PHILADELPHIA** Cream
   Cheese, softened
1 jar (7 oz.) **JET-PUFFED**
   Marshmallow Creme

MIX ingredients until well blended; cover.

REFRIGERATE until ready to serve.

SERVE with assorted **NABISCO** Cookies or cut-up fresh fruit.

Makes: 14 servings,
2 Tbsp. each.

MALLOW FRUIT DIP: Add 1 Tbsp. orange juice, 1 tsp. grated orange peel and a dash of ground ginger.

HOW TO SOFTEN CREAM CHEESE: Place completely unwrapped package of cream cheese on microwaveable plate. Microwave on HIGH 10 to 15 seconds or until slightly softened.

MAKE IT EASY: To easily remove marshmallow creme from jar, remove lid and seal. Microwave on HIGH 30 seconds.

New York-Style Sour Cream-Topped Cheesecake

PREP: 15 MIN. PLUS REFRIGERATING • BAKE: 40 MIN.

1½ cups **HONEY MAID** Graham Cracker
    Crumbs
¼ cup (½ stick) butter, melted
1¼ cups sugar, divided
4 pkg. (8 oz. each) **PHILADELPHIA**
   Cream Cheese, softened
2 tsp. vanilla, divided
1 container (16 oz.) **BREAKSTONE'S** or
   KNUDSEN Sour Cream, divided
4 eggs

PREHEAT oven to 325°F. Line 13×9-inch baking pan with foil, with ends of foil extending over sides of pan. Mix crumbs, butter and 2 Tbsp. of the sugar; press firmly onto bottom of prepared pan.

BEAT cream cheese, 1 cup of the remaining sugar and 1 tsp. of the vanilla in large bowl with electric mixer on medium speed until well blended. Add 1 cup of the sour cream; mix well. Add eggs, 1 at a time, beating on low speed after each addition just until blended. Pour over crust.

BAKE 40 min. or until center is almost set. Mix remaining sour cream, 2 Tbsp. sugar and 1 tsp. vanilla until well blended; carefully spread over cheesecake. Bake an additional 10 min. Cool. Cover; refrigerate 4 hours or overnight. Lift cheesecake from pan, using foil handles. Garnish as desired. Store leftover cheesecake in refrigerator.

Makes: 16 servings, 1 piece each.

Tiramisu Cheesecake

White Chocolate Cheesecake

Tiramisu Cheesecake

PREP: 20 MIN. PLUS REFRIGERATING • BAKE: 45 MIN.

1 box (12 oz.) **NILLA** Wafers (about 88 wafers), divided

5 tsp. **MAXWELL HOUSE** Instant Coffee, divided

3 Tbsp. hot water, divided

4 pkg. (8 oz. each) **PHILADELPHIA** Cream Cheese, softened

1 cup sugar

1 cup **BREAKSTONE'S** or **KNUDSEN** Sour Cream

4 eggs

1 cup thawed **COOL WHIP** Whipped Topping

2 Tbsp. unsweetened cocoa powder

PREHEAT oven to 325°F. Line 13×9-inch baking pan with foil, with ends of foil extending over sides of pan. Layer half of the wafers (about 44) on bottom of prepared pan. Dissolve 2 tsp. of the coffee granules in 2 Tbsp. of the hot water. Brush wafers with half of the dissolved coffee mixture; set remaining aside.

BEAT cream cheese and sugar in large bowl with electric mixer on medium speed until well blended. Add sour cream; mix well. Add eggs, 1 at a time, mixing on low speed after each addition just until blended. Dissolve remaining 3 tsp. coffee granules in remaining 1 Tbsp. hot water. Remove 3½ cups of the batter; place in medium bowl. Stir in dissolved coffee. Pour coffee-flavored batter over wafers in baking pan. Layer remaining wafers over batter. Brush wafers with reserved dissolved coffee. Pour remaining plain batter over wafers.

BAKE 45 min. or until center is almost set. Cool. Refrigerate 3 hours or overnight. Lift cheesecake from pan, using foil handles. Spread with whipped topping; sprinkle with cocoa. Cut into 16 pieces to serve. Store leftover cheesecake in refrigerator.

Makes: 16 servings, 1 piece each.

White Chocolate Cheesecake

PREP: 30 MIN. PLUS REFRIGERATING • BAKE: 1 HOUR

¾ cup sugar, divided

½ cup (1 stick) butter, softened

1½ tsp. vanilla, divided

1 cup all-purpose flour

4 pkg. (8 oz. each) **PHILADELPHIA** Cream Cheese, softened

2 pkg. (6 squares each) **BAKER'S** Premium White Baking Chocolate, melted, slightly cooled

4 eggs

1 pt. (2 cups) raspberries

PREHEAT oven to 325°F if using a silver 9-inch springform pan (or to 300°F if using a dark nonstick 9-inch springform pan). Beat ¼ cup of the sugar, the butter and ½ tsp. of the vanilla in small bowl with electric mixer on medium speed until light and fluffy. Gradually add flour, mixing on low speed until well blended after each addition. Press firmly onto bottom of pan; prick with fork. Bake 25 min. or until edge is lightly browned.

BEAT cream cheese, remaining ½ cup sugar and remaining 1 tsp. vanilla in large bowl with electric mixer on medium speed until well blended. Add melted chocolate; mix well. Add eggs, 1 at a time, beating on low speed after each addition just until blended. Pour over crust.

BAKE 55 min. to 1 hour or until center is almost set. Run knife or metal spatula around rim of pan to loosen cake; cool before removing rim of pan. Refrigerate 4 hours or overnight. Top with the raspberries just before serving. Store leftover cheesecake in refrigerator.

Makes: 16 servings.

Apple Pecan Cheesecake

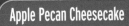

Chocolate Royale Cheesecake Squares

Apple Pecan Cheesecake

PREP: 15 MIN. PLUS REFRIGERATING • BAKE: 55 MIN.

- 1½ cups **HONEY MAID** Graham Cracker Crumbs
- ¼ cup (½ stick) butter, melted
- 2 Tbsp. firmly packed brown sugar
- 4 pkg. (8 oz. each) **PHILADELPHIA** Cream Cheese, softened
- 1½ cups firmly packed brown sugar, divided
- 1 tsp. vanilla
- 1 cup **BREAKSTONE'S** or **KNUDSEN** Sour Cream
- 4 eggs
- 4 cups chopped peeled apples (about 3 medium)
- ¾ cup **PLANTERS** Chopped Pecans
- 1 tsp. ground cinnamon

PREHEAT oven to 325°F. Line 13×9-inch baking pan with foil, with ends of foil extending over sides of pan. Mix crumbs, butter and 2 Tbsp. brown sugar; press firmly onto bottom of pan.

BEAT cream cheese, 1 cup of the brown sugar and the vanilla in large bowl with electric mixer on medium speed until well blended. Add sour cream; mix well. Add eggs, 1 at a time, mixing on low speed after each addition just until blended. Pour over crust. Mix remaining ½ cup brown sugar, the apples, pecans and cinnamon; spoon evenly over cheesecake batter.

BAKE 55 min. or until center is almost set. Cool. Refrigerate 4 hours or overnight. Let stand at room temperature 30 min. before serving. Lift cheesecake from pan, using foil handles. Cut into 16 pieces. Store leftover cheesecake in refrigerator.

Makes: 16 servings, 1 piece each.

Chocolate Royale Cheesecake Squares

PREP: 20 MIN. PLUS REFRIGERATING • BAKE: 50 MIN.

- 24 **OREO** Chocolate Sandwich Cookies, crushed (about 2 cups)
- ¼ cup (½ stick) butter or margarine, melted
- 4 pkg. (8 oz. each) **PHILADELPHIA** Cream Cheese, softened
- 1 cup sugar
- 2 Tbsp. all-purpose flour
- 1 tsp. vanilla
- 1 pkg. (8 squares) **BAKER'S** Semi-Sweet Baking Chocolate, melted, slightly cooled
- 4 eggs

PREHEAT oven to 325°F. Mix crumbs and butter; press firmly onto bottom of 13×9-inch baking pan. Bake 10 min.

BEAT cream cheese, sugar, flour and vanilla in large bowl with electric mixer on medium speed until well blended. Add melted chocolate; mix well. Add eggs, 1 at a time, mixing on low speed after each addition just until blended. Pour over crust.

BAKE 45 to 50 min. or until center is almost set. Refrigerate at least 4 hours or overnight. Cut into 32 squares to serve. Store leftover dessert squares in refrigerator.

Makes: 32 servings, 1 square each.

Ribbon Bar Cheesecake

PHILLY Blueberry Swirl Cheesecake

Ribbon Bar Cheesecake

PREP: 15 MIN. PLUS REFRIGERATING • BAKE: 40 MIN.

30 **OREO** Chocolate Sandwich Cookies,
      crushed
½ cup (1 stick) butter, melted
¼ cup **PLANTERS** Chopped Pecans
¼ cup **BAKER'S ANGEL FLAKE** Coconut
4 pkg. (8 oz. each) **PHILADELPHIA**
      Cream Cheese, softened
1 cup sugar
4 eggs
½ cup whipping cream
6 squares **BAKER'S** Semi-Sweet Baking
      Chocolate

PREHEAT oven to 350°F. Mix crushed cookies,
butter, pecans and coconut; press firmly onto
bottom of 13×9-inch baking pan. Refrigerate
while preparing filling.

BEAT cream cheese and sugar in large bowl
with electric mixer on medium speed until well
blended. Add eggs, 1 at a time, mixing on low
speed after each addition just until blended.
Pour over crust.

BAKE 40 min. or until center is almost set.
Cool. Refrigerate 3 hours or overnight. Place
whipping cream and chocolate in saucepan.
Cook on low heat until chocolate is completely
melted and mixture is well blended, stirring
occasionally. Pour over cheesecake. Refrigerate
15 min. or until chocolate is firm. Store leftover
cheesecake in refrigerator.

Makes: 16 servings, 1 square each.

SIZE-WISE: This party-size cheesecake is great
for large crowds. Be mindful of serving size.

JAZZ IT UP: After chocolate topping is
firm, place 1 additional chocolate square in
microwaveable bowl. Microwave on MEDIUM
1 min., stirring after 30 seconds. Stir until
chocolate is completely melted. Pour into
small resealable bag; seal bag. Snip off one
small corner from bottom of bag; twist top of
bag to squeeze chocolate from bag to pipe a
special message, such as "Greetings," on top of
cheesecake.

PHILLY Blueberry Swirl Cheesecake

PREP: 15 MIN. PLUS REFRIGERATING • BAKE: 45 MIN.

1 cup **HONEY MAID** Graham Cracker
      Crumbs
1 cup plus 3 Tbsp. sugar, divided
3 Tbsp. butter or margarine, melted
4 pkg. (8 oz. each) **PHILADELPHIA**
      Cream Cheese, softened
1 tsp. vanilla
1 cup **BREAKSTONE'S** or **KNUDSEN**
      Sour Cream
4 eggs
2 cups fresh or thawed frozen
      blueberries

PREHEAT oven to 325°F. Mix crumbs, 3 Tbsp.
of the sugar and the butter. Press firmly onto
bottom of foil-lined 13×9-inch baking pan.
Bake 10 min.

BEAT cream cheese, remaining 1 cup sugar and
the vanilla in large bowl with electric mixer on
medium speed until well blended. Add sour
cream; mix well. Add eggs, 1 at a time, beating
on low speed after each addition just until
blended. Pour over crust. Purée the blueberries
in a blender or food processor. Gently drop
spoonfuls of the puréed blueberries over batter;
cut through batter several times with knife for
marble effect.

BAKE 45 min. or until center is almost set;
cool. Refrigerate at least 4 hours or overnight.
Garnish as desired. Store leftover cheesecake in
refrigerator.

Makes: 16 servings.

PHILADELPHIA Classic Cheesecake

Our Best Chocolate Cheesecake

PHILADELPHIA Classic Cheesecake

PREP: 20 MIN. PLUS REFRIGERATING • BAKE: 55 MIN.

1½ cups **HONEY MAID** Graham Cracker Crumbs
3 Tbsp. sugar
⅓ cup butter or margarine, melted
4 pkg. (8 oz. each) **PHILADELPHIA** Cream Cheese, softened
1 cup sugar
1 tsp. vanilla
4 eggs

PREHEAT oven to 325°F if using a silver 9-inch springform pan (or to 300°F if using a dark nonstick springform pan). Mix crumbs, 3 Tbsp. sugar and butter; press firmly onto bottom of pan.

BEAT cream cheese, 1 cup sugar and vanilla with electric mixer on medium speed until well blended. Add eggs, 1 at a time, mixing on low speed after each addition just until blended. Pour over crust.

BAKE 55 min. or until center is almost set. Loosen cake from side of pan; cool before removing side of pan. Refrigerate 4 hours or overnight. Store leftover cheesecake in refrigerator.

Makes: 16 servings.

SIZE IT UP: Sweets can add enjoyment to a balanced diet, but remember to keep tabs on portions.

SPECIAL EXTRA: Top with fresh fruit just before serving.

Our Best Chocolate Cheesecake

PREP: 30 MIN. PLUS REFRIGERATING • BAKE: 55 MIN.

1½ cups crushed **OREO** Chocolate Sandwich Cookies (about 18 cookies)
2 Tbsp. butter or margarine, melted
3 pkg. (8 oz. each) **PHILADELPHIA** Cream Cheese, softened
1 cup sugar
1 tsp. vanilla
1 pkg. (8 squares) **BAKER'S** Semi-Sweet Baking Chocolate, melted, slightly cooled
3 eggs
1 cup thawed **COOL WHIP** Strawberry Whipped Topping
1½ cups assorted seasonal fruit, such as chopped strawberries and sliced kiwi

PREHEAT oven to 325°F if using a silver 9-inch springform pan (or to 300°F if using a dark nonstick 9-inch springform pan). Mix crushed cookies and butter; press firmly onto bottom of pan. Bake 10 min.

BEAT cream cheese, sugar and vanilla with electric mixer on medium speed until well blended. Add chocolate; mix well. Add eggs, 1 at a time, mixing on low speed after each addition just until blended. Pour over crust.

BAKE 45 to 55 min. or until center is almost set. Run knife or metal spatula around rim of pan to loosen cake; cool before removing rim of pan. Refrigerate 4 hours or overnight. Top with whipped topping and fruit.

Makes: 16 servings.

SIZE-WISE: Looking for a special treat? 1 serving of this cheesecake is full of chocolatey flavor.

HOW TO SOFTEN CREAM CHEESE: Place completely unwrapped pkg. of cream cheese in microwaveable bowl. Microwave on HIGH 45 sec. or until slightly softened.

HOW TO: This recipe can also be made in a greased, foil-lined 13×9-inch baking pan. Reduce the baking time by 5 to 10 min.

PHILADELPHIA Blueberry No-Bake Cheesecake

Creamy Strawberry Cookie "Tarts"

PHILADELPHIA Blueberry No-Bake Cheesecake

PREP: 15 MIN. PLUS REFRIGERATING

2 cups **HONEY MAID** Graham Cracker Crumbs
6 Tbsp. margarine, melted
1 cup sugar, divided
4 pkg. (8 oz. each) **PHILADELPHIA** Neufchâtel Cheese, ⅓ Less Fat than Cream Cheese, softened
½ cup blueberry preserves
  Grated peel from 1 lemon
1 pkg. (16 oz.) frozen blueberries, thawed, drained
1 tub (8 oz.) **COOL WHIP LITE** Whipped Topping, thawed

MIX graham crumbs, margarine and ¼ cup of the sugar; press firmly onto bottom of 13×9-inch pan. Refrigerate while preparing filling.

BEAT Neufchâtel cheese and remaining ¾ cup sugar in large bowl with electric mixer on medium speed until well blended. Add preserves and lemon peel, mix until blended. Stir in blueberries. Gently stir in whipped topping. Spoon over crust; cover.

REFRIGERATE 4 hours or until firm. Garnish as desired. Store leftovers in refrigerator.

HOW TO MAKE IT WITH FRESH BLUEBERRIES: Place 2 cups blueberries in small bowl with 2 Tbsp. sugar; mash with fork. Add to Neufchâtel cheese mixture; continue as directed.

Makes: 16 servings, 1 piece each.

Creamy Strawberry Cookie "Tarts"

PREP: 15 MIN. PLUS REFRIGERATING

⅔ cup boiling water
1 pkg. (4-serving size) **JELL-O** Brand Strawberry Flavor Gelatin
1 pkg. (8 oz.) **PHILADELPHIA** Cream Cheese, cubed
1 cup thawed **COOL WHIP** Whipped Topping
12 **CHIPS AHOY!** Real Chocolate Chip Cookies
12 small strawberries

STIR boiling water into dry gelatin mix in small bowl at least 2 min. until completely dissolved. Cool 5 min., stirring occasionally.

POUR gelatin mixture into blender. Add cream cheese; cover. Blend on medium speed 30 to 45 sec. or until well blended; scrape down side of blender container, if needed. Add whipped topping; cover. Blend on low speed 5 sec. or just until blended.

LINE 12 muffin pan cups with paper liners; spray with cooking spray. Place 1 cookie on bottom of each prepared cup; top evenly with the gelatin mixture. Refrigerate 1 hour 30 min. or until firm. Top each with a strawberry just before serving. Store leftover desserts in refrigerator.

Makes: 12 servings.

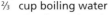

PHILADELPHIA Chocolate Cheesecakes For Two

Chocolate & Peanut Butter Ribbon Dessert

PHILADELPHIA Chocolate Cheesecakes For Two

PREP: 10 MIN. PLUS REFRIGERATING

2 oz. (¼ of 8-oz. pkg.) **PHILADELPHIA** Cream Cheese, softened
1 Tbsp. sugar
1 square **BAKER'S** Semi-Sweet Baking Chocolate, melted
½ cup thawed **COOL WHIP** Whipped Topping
2 **OREO** Chocolate Sandwich Cookies

BEAT cream cheese, sugar and chocolate in medium bowl with wire whisk until well blended. Add whipped topping; mix well.

PLACE 1 cookie on bottom of each of 2 paper-lined medium muffin cups; fill evenly with cream cheese mixture.

REFRIGERATE 2 hours or overnight. (Or, if you are in a hurry, place in the freezer for 1 hour.)

JAZZ IT UP: Dust surface with cocoa powder. Top with heart-shaped stencil; dust with powdered sugar.

Makes: 2 servings.

Chocolate & Peanut Butter Ribbon Dessert

PREP: 15 MIN. PLUS REFRIGERATING

12 **NUTTER BUTTER** Peanut Butter Sandwich Cookies, divided
2 Tbsp. butter, melted
1 pkg. (8 oz.) **PHILADELPHIA** Cream Cheese, softened
½ cup creamy peanut butter
½ cup sugar
2 tsp. vanilla
1 tub (12 oz.) **COOL WHIP** Whipped Topping, thawed, divided
2 squares **BAKER'S** Semi-Sweet Baking Chocolate, melted

CRUSH 8 of the cookies in resealable plastic bag with rolling pin. Mix cookie crumbs and butter. Press onto bottom of foil-lined 9×5-inch loaf pan.

MIX cream cheese, peanut butter, sugar and vanilla with electric mixer on medium speed until well blended. Gently stir in 3 cups of the whipped topping. Spoon ½ cup of the cream cheese mixture into small bowl. Stir in melted chocolate until well blended; set aside. Spoon half of the remaining cream cheese mixture over crust. Top evenly with chocolate mixture; cover with remaining cream cheese mixture.

FREEZE 4 hours or overnight until firm. Invert onto plate. Remove foil, then re-invert onto serving platter so that crumb layer is on bottom. Coarsely break the remaining 4 cookies. Top dessert with remaining whipping topping and cookies.

Makes: 12 servings.

Tiramisu Bowl

Strawberry Freeze

Tiramisu Bowl

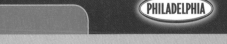

PREP: 20 MIN. PLUS REFRIGERATING

1 pkg. (8 oz.) **PHILADELPHIA** Cream Cheese, softened

3 cups cold milk

2 pkg. (4-serving size each) **JELL-O** Vanilla Flavor Instant Pudding & Pie Filling

1 tub (8 oz.) **COOL WHIP** Whipped Topping, thawed, divided

48 **NILLA** Wafers

½ cup brewed strong **MAXWELL HOUSE** Coffee, cooled

2 squares **BAKER'S** Semi-Sweet Baking Chocolate, coarsely grated

1 cup fresh raspberries

BEAT cream cheese in large bowl with electric mixer until creamy. Gradually beat in milk. Add dry pudding mixes; mix well. Stir in 2 cups of the whipped topping.

LINE bottom and sides of a 2½-qt. bowl with half of the wafers; drizzle with half of the coffee. Layer half of the pudding mixture over wafers, and then top with half of the grated chocolate. Repeat all layers starting with the wafers and coffee. Top with remaining whipped topping and raspberries.

REFRIGERATE at least 2 hours. Store leftovers in refrigerator.

Makes: 16 servings, about ⅔ cup each.

Strawberry Freeze

PREP: 15 MIN. PLUS REFRIGERATING

12 **CHIPS AHOY!** Real Chocolate Chip Cookies

1 pkg. (8 oz.) **PHILADELPHIA** Cream Cheese, softened

½ cup sugar

1 can (12 oz.) frozen berry juice concentrate, thawed

1 cup crushed strawberries

1 tub (8 oz.) **COOL WHIP** Whipped Topping, thawed

2 cups strawberries, halved

ARRANGE cookies in single layer on bottom of 9-inch springform pan; set aside.

BEAT cream cheese and sugar in large bowl with electric mixer on medium speed until well blended. Gradually add juice concentrate, beating well after each addition. Stir in crushed strawberries. Add whipped topping; stir with wire whisk until well blended. Pour over cookies in pan.

FREEZE 6 hours or until firm. Remove from freezer; let stand in refrigerator 15 min. to soften slightly. Top with the halved strawberries just before serving. Store leftover dessert in freezer.

Makes: 16 servings.

SUBSTITUTE: Prepare as directed, using COOL WHIP Strawberry Whipped Topping.

HEALTHY LIVING: Trim 4 grams of fat and 2 grams of saturated fat per serving by preparing with CHIPS AHOY! Reduced Fat Real Chocolate Chip Cookies; PHILADELPHIA Neufchâtel Cheese, ⅓ Less Fat than Cream Cheese and COOL WHIP LITE Whipped Topping.

SUBSTITUTE: Prepare as directed, using your favorite flavor of frozen juice or drink concentrate, such as raspberry, lemonade, grape or pink lemonade.

Fluffy 2-STEP Cheesecake Minis

Lem'n Berry Cheesecake

Fluffy 2-STEP Cheesecake Minis

PREP: 10 MIN. PLUS REFRIGERATING

12 **NILLA** Wafers
1 pkg. (8 oz.) **PHILADELPHIA** Cream Cheese, softened
⅓ cup sugar
1 tub (8 oz.) **COOL WHIP** Whipped Topping, thawed, divided
¼ cup **BAKER'S ANGEL FLAKE** Coconut, toasted

PLACE 1 wafer on bottom of each of 12 paper-lined medium muffin cups; set aside. Beat cream cheese and sugar in large bowl with wire whisk or electric mixer until well blended. Add 2¼ cups of the whipped topping; mix well. Spoon evenly into muffin cups.

REFRIGERATE 3 hours or overnight. Spread tops with remaining whipped topping. Sprinkle with coconut just before serving. Store leftover cheesecakes in refrigerator.

Makes: 12 servings,
1 cheesecake each.

Lem'n Berry Cheesecake

PREP: 10 MIN. PLUS REFRIGERATING

1 pkg. (8 oz.) **PHILADELPHIA** Cream Cheese, softened
¼ cup **COUNTRY TIME** Lemonade Flavor Drink Mix
2 Tbsp. sugar
½ cup milk
2 cups thawed **COOL WHIP** Whipped Topping
1 **HONEY MAID** Graham Pie Crust (6 oz.)
1 cup assorted fresh berries

BEAT cream cheese, drink mix and sugar in large bowl until well blended. Gradually add milk, mixing until well blended. Gently stir in whipped topping.

SPOON into crust.

REFRIGERATE 1 hour or until ready to serve. Garnish with berries.

Makes: 8 servings.

GREAT SUBSTITUTE: Prepare as directed, using PHILADELPHIA Neufchâtel Cheese, ⅓ Less Fat than Cream Cheese and COOL WHIP LITE Whipped Topping.

Easy Chocolate Truffles

Zesty Chicken Pot Pie

PHILADELPHIA

Easy Chocolate Truffles

PREP: 30 MIN. PLUS REFRIGERATING

1 pkg. (8 oz.) **PHILADELPHIA** Cream Cheese, softened

3 cups powdered sugar

1½ pkg. (12 squares) **BAKER'S** Semi-Sweet Baking Chocolate, melted

1½ tsp. vanilla

Suggested coatings: ground **PLANTERS** Walnuts, unsweetened cocoa, powdered sugar and/or **BAKER'S ANGEL FLAKE** Coconut

BEAT cream cheese in large bowl with electric mixer on medium speed until smooth. Gradually add sugar, mixing until well blended.

ADD melted chocolate and vanilla; mix well. Refrigerate 1 hour or until chilled.

SHAPE into 1-inch balls. Roll in walnuts, cocoa, powdered sugar or coconut. Store in refrigerator.

Makes: 24 servings, 3 truffles each.

SIZE-WISE: Put these truffles in pretty fluted candy cups and display on a silver platter for an elegant presentation. Each one is a very special treat. Enjoy a serving after dinner with a cup of freshly brewed coffee.

EASY SPIRITED CHOCOLATE TRUFFLES: Prepare as directed except omit vanilla. Divide truffle mixture into thirds. Add 1 Tbsp. liqueur (almond, coffee or orange-flavored) to each third of mixture; mix well.

PHILADELPHIA

Zesty Chicken Pot Pie

PREP: 20 MIN. • BAKE: 25 MIN.

12 oz. (1½ pkg. [8 oz. each]) **PHILADELPHIA** Cream Cheese, cubed

½ cup chicken broth

3 cups chopped cooked chicken

2 pkg. (10 oz. each) frozen mixed vegetables, thawed

1 env. **GOOD SEASONS** Italian Salad Dressing & Recipe Mix

1 refrigerated ready-to-use refrigerated pie crust (½ of 15-oz. pkg.)

PREHEAT oven to 425°F. Place cream cheese in large saucepan. Add broth; cook on low heat until cream cheese is completely melted, stirring frequently with wire whisk. Stir in chicken, vegetables and salad dressing mix.

SPOON into 9-inch pie plate. Cover with pie crust; seal and flute edge. Cut several slits in crust to allow steam to escape. Place pie plate on baking sheet.

BAKE 20 to 25 min. or until golden brown.

Makes: 8 servings.

SERVING SUGGESTION: Serve with a mixed green salad and glass of fat-free milk.

MAKE AHEAD: Prepare as directed except for baking. Wrap securely; freeze. When ready to bake, unwrap. Place strips of foil around edge to prevent over browning. Bake frozen pie at 425°F for 1 hour and 10 min. or until heated through.

SUBSTITUTES: Prepare as directed, using PHILADELPHIA Neufchâtel Cheese, ⅓ Less Fat than Cream Cheese, OR GOOD SEASONS Zesty Italian Dressing OR substituting turkey for the chicken.

Family-Favorite Roast Chicken

Diner Special Meatloaf

Family-Favorite Roast Chicken

PREP: 10 MIN. • BAKE: 1 HOUR 30 MIN.

1   (4½-lb.) roasting chicken
¼   tsp. black pepper
⅛   tsp. salt
1   medium lemon, washed
4   oz. (½ of 8-oz. pkg.) **PHILADELPHIA** Cream Cheese, softened
1   Tbsp. Italian seasoning
½   cup **KRAFT** Zesty Italian Dressing

PREHEAT oven to 350°F. Rinse chicken; pat dry with paper towel. Use the tip of a sharp knife to separate the chicken skin from the meat in the chicken breast and tops of the legs. Sprinkle chicken both inside and out with the pepper and salt. Place in 13×9-inch baking dish.

GRATE the lemon; mix the peel with cream cheese and Italian seasoning. Use a small spoon or your fingers to carefully stuff the cream cheese mixture under the chicken skin, pushing the cream cheese mixture carefully toward the legs, being careful to not tear the skin.

CUT the lemon in half; squeeze both halves into small bowl. Add dressing; beat with wire whisk until well blended. Drizzle evenly over chicken. Place the squeezed lemon halves inside the chicken cavity. Insert an ovenproof meat thermometer into thickest part of 1 of the chicken's thighs.

BAKE 1 hour 30 min. or until chicken is no longer pink in center (165°F), basting occasionally with the pan juices.

Makes: 8 servings.

Diner Special Meatloaf

PREP: 15 MIN. • BAKE: 55 MIN.

1   lb. lean ground beef
½   cup **KRAFT** Original Barbecue Sauce
½   cup dry bread crumbs
1   egg, lightly beaten
1¼   cups water
¾   cup milk
2   Tbsp. butter or margarine
½   tsp. salt
1½   cups instant potato flakes
3   oz. **PHILADELPHIA** Cream Cheese, cubed
2   **KRAFT** Singles

PREHEAT oven to 375°F. Mix meat, barbecue sauce, bread crumbs and egg. Shape into loaf in 12×8-inch baking dish.

BAKE 55 minutes. Meanwhile, bring water to boil in medium saucepan. Add milk, butter and salt; stir in potato flakes. Add cream cheese; stir until completely melted.

SPREAD potato mixture over meatloaf; top with Singles. Bake an additional 5 minutes or until Singles begin to melt.

Makes: 4 servings.

ROUND OUT THE MEAL: Serve with a steamed green vegetable, such as green beans, and a whole wheat roll.

GREAT SUBSTITUTE: Substitute 1 pkg. (16 oz.) frozen LOUIS RICH Ground Turkey for the ground beef.

SPECIAL EXTRA: Garnish with chopped fresh chives just before serving.

20-Minute Skillet Salmon

Pasta Primavera Alfredo

20-Minute Skillet Salmon

PHILADELPHIA

PREP: 10 MIN. • COOK: 10 MIN.

1 Tbsp. oil
4 salmon fillets (1 lb.)
1 cup fat-free milk
½ cup (½ of 8-oz. tub) **PHILADELPHIA** Light Cream Cheese Spread
½ cup chopped cucumbers
2 Tbsp. chopped fresh dill

HEAT oil in large skillet on medium-high heat. Add salmon; cook 5 min. on each side or until salmon flakes easily with fork. Remove from skillet; cover to keep warm.

ADD milk and cream cheese spread to skillet; cook and stir until cream cheese spread is melted and mixture is well blended. Stir in cucumbers and dill.

RETURN salmon to skillet. Cook 2 min. or until heated through. Serve salmon topped with the cream cheese sauce.

Makes: 4 servings.

COOKING KNOW-HOW: When salmon is done, it will appear opaque and flake easily with fork.

FOOD FACTS: Check salmon fillets for bones before cooking by running fingers over surface. Small bumps are usually a sign of bones. Use tweezers to remove any bones.

SUBSTITUTE: Substitute 2 tsp. dill weed for the 2 Tbsp. chopped fresh dill.

Pasta Primavera Alfredo

PHILADELPHIA

PREP: 5 MIN. • COOK: 15 MIN.

4 oz. (½ of 8-oz. pkg.) **PHILADELPHIA** Cream Cheese, cubed
¾ cup milk
½ cup **KRAFT** Shredded Parmesan Cheese
¼ cup (½ stick) butter or margarine
¼ tsp. white pepper
¼ tsp. garlic powder
⅛ tsp. ground nutmeg
2 cups small broccoli florets
1 cup chopped carrots
1 pkg. (9 oz.) refrigerated fettuccine

PLACE cream cheese, milk, Parmesan cheese and butter in small saucepan; cook on medium-low heat until cream cheese is completely melted and mixture is well blended, stirring occasionally. Add pepper, garlic powder and nutmeg; stir until well blended.

MEANWHILE, add vegetables and pasta to 2½ qt. boiling water in large saucepan; cook 3 min. Drain.

TOSS pasta mixture with the cream cheese mixture.

Makes: 5 servings, 1¼ cups each.

Stuffed Fiesta Burgers

Creamy Bow-Tie Pasta With Chicken And Broccoli

Stuffed Fiesta Burgers

PREP: 15 MIN. • GRILL: 9 MIN.

1 lb. ground beef
1 pkg. (1¼ oz.) **TACO BELL® HOME ORIGINALS®** Taco Seasoning Mix
¼ cup **PHILADELPHIA** Chive & Onion Cream Cheese Spread
⅓ cup **KRAFT** Shredded Cheddar Cheese
4 hamburger buns, split, lightly toasted
½ cup **TACO BELL® HOME ORIGINALS®** Thick 'N Chunky Medium Salsa
1 avocado, peeled, pitted and cut into 8 slices

PREHEAT grill to medium heat. Mix meat and seasoning mix. Shape into 8 thin patties. Mix cream cheese spread and shredded cheese. Spoon about 2 Tbsp. of the cheese mixture onto center of each of 4 of the patties; top with second patty. Pinch edges of patties together to seal.

GRILL 7 to 9 min. on each side or until cooked through (160°F).

COVER bottom halves of buns with burgers. Top with salsa, avocado slices and top halves of buns.

Makes: 4 servings, 1 burger each.

TACO BELL® and HOME ORIGINALS® are trademarks owned and licensed by Taco Bell Corp.

Creamy Bow-Tie Pasta With Chicken And Broccoli

PREP: 10 MIN. • COOK: 15 MIN.

3 cups (8 oz.) farfalle (bow-tie pasta), uncooked
4 cups broccoli florets
3 Tbsp. **KRAFT** Roasted Red Pepper Italian with Parmesan Dressing
6 small boneless, skinless chicken breast halves (1½ lb.)
2 cloves garlic, minced
2 cups tomato-basil spaghetti sauce
4 oz. (½ of 8-oz. pkg.) **PHILADELPHIA** Neufchâtel Cheese, ⅓ Less Fat than Cream Cheese, cubed
¼ cup **KRAFT** 100% Grated Parmesan Cheese

COOK pasta as directed on package, adding broccoli to the cooking water for the last 3 min. of the pasta cooking time. Meanwhile, heat dressing in large nonstick skillet on medium heat. Add chicken and garlic; cook 5 min. Turn chicken over; continue cooking 4 to 5 min. or until chicken is cooked through (170°F).

DRAIN pasta mixture in colander; return to pan and set aside. Add spaghetti sauce and Neufchâtel cheese to chicken in skillet; cook on medium-low heat 2 to 3 min. or until Neufchâtel cheese is completely melted, mixture is well blended and chicken is coated with sauce, stirring occasionally. Remove chicken from skillet; keep warm. Add sauce mixture to pasta mixture; mix well. Transfer to 6 serving bowls.

CUT chicken crosswise into thick slices; fan out chicken over pasta mixture. Sprinkle evenly with Parmesan cheese.

Makes: 6 servings, about 1½ cups each.

SUBSTITUTE: Prepare as directed, using whole wheat or multigrain pasta.

Spaghetti With Zesty Bolognese

Chicken Enchiladas

Spaghetti With Zesty Bolognese

PREP: 10 MIN. • COOK: 15 MIN.

1 small onion, chopped
¼ cup **KRAFT** Light Zesty Italian Reduced Fat Dressing
1 lb. extra lean ground beef
1 can (15 oz.) tomato sauce
1 can (14 oz.) diced tomatoes, undrained
2 Tbsp. **PHILADELPHIA** Neufchâtel Cheese, ⅓ Less Fat than Cream Cheese
12 oz. spaghetti, uncooked
¼ cup **KRAFT** 100% Grated Parmesan Cheese

COOK onions in dressing in large skillet on medium heat. Increase heat to medium-high. Add meat; cook, stirring frequently, until browned. Stir in tomato sauce and tomatoes. Bring to boil. Reduce heat to medium-low; simmer 15 min. Remove from heat. Stir in Neufchâtel cheese until well blended.

MEANWHILE, cook pasta as directed on package.

SPOON sauce over pasta. Sprinkle with Parmesan cheese.

Makes: 6 servings.

Chicken Enchiladas

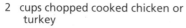

PREP: 20 MIN. • BAKE: 20 MIN.

2 cups chopped cooked chicken or turkey
1 green bell pepper, chopped
4 oz. (½ of 8-oz. pkg.) **PHILADELPHIA** Cream Cheese, cubed
½ cup **TACO BELL® HOME ORIGINALS®** Thick 'N Chunky Salsa, divided
8 **TACO BELL® HOME ORIGINALS®** Flour Tortillas
¼ lb. (4 oz.) **VELVEETA** Pasteurized Prepared Cheese Product, cut into ½-inch cubes
1 Tbsp. milk

PREHEAT oven to 350°F. Mix chicken, green bell pepper, cream cheese and ¼ cup of the salsa in saucepan; cook on low heat until cream cheese is melted, stirring occasionally.

SPOON ⅓ cup of the chicken mixture down center of each tortilla; roll up. Place, seam-sides down, in lightly greased 13×9-inch baking dish. Place **VELVEETA** in small saucepan. Add milk; cook on low heat until **VELVEETA** is completely melted, stirring frequently. Pour over enchiladas; cover with foil.

BAKE 20 min. or until heated through. Top with remaining ¼ cup salsa.

Makes: 4 servings, 2 enchiladas each.

TACO BELL® and HOME ORIGINALS® are trademarks owned and licensed by Taco Bell Corp.

SUBSTITUTE: Prepare as directed, using PHILADELPHIA Neufchâtel Cheese, ⅓ Less Fat than Cream Cheese and VELVEETA Made With 2% Milk Reduced Fat Pasteurized Prepared Cheese Product.

SHORTCUT: Substitute 1 pkg. (6 oz.) OSCAR MAYER Oven Roasted Chicken Breast Cuts for the chopped cooked fresh chicken.